Convictions

A Historical Romance Novel

Sylvia Melvin

This is a work of historical fiction based on the American Civil War. The names of historical people, battles, events, etc., are real. The plot and characters are fictitious, and any resemblance to actual persons, living or dead, locales or events is entirely coincidental.

Copyright © 2015 Sylvia Melvin

ISBN: 1508569320
EAN-13: 978-1508569329

Sincerely,
Sylvia Melvin

Acknowledgments

As I delved into researching material for "Convictions", whether examining static displays in the Civil War Museum in Harrisburg, Pennsylvania, walking the battle fields at Gettysburg, reading numerous books, articles or soldiers' letters, one thought prevailed: The convictions of those involved in the Civil War ran deep. So deep that they were willing to sever family ties and put their lives on the line.

In reading this book, I hope the sacrifice rings clear and we might ask ourselves the question: Would I have done the same?

As in writing the past six novels, I appreciate the help and support given me to accomplish my goal. The following thanks to:

Members of the Panhandle Writer's Group- You challenged me to listen to suggestions, rewrite when necessary and praised my efforts.

Robert Howard- The multiple books you loaned me from your Civil War library provided true insight into the minds of the men who fought on the field.

Toni New- Your artistic talent is so evident in the outstanding cover design.

Al Melvin- The encouragement you give me is appreciated beyond words.

My faithful followers- I trust I've met your expectations.

Sincerely,
Sylvia

Also By Sylvia Melvin

Biography:

Helena: Unwavering Courage
Southern Sage: The Honorable Woodrow Melvin

Mystery:

Death Behind the Dunes
Death Beyond the Breaakers
Death On Blackwater Bay

Romance:

Summer Guest

Chapter One

July 3, 1863

    Confederate cannons boomed sending exploding shells in all directions. Thick clouds of white smoke blanketed the area. Screams from wounded men, and the firing of muskets added to the pandemonium. Meadowlarks no longer flew across the partially clouded sky. Frightened rabbits scurried into the woods, diving into their burrows. A doe and her fawn, confused by the surrounding unfamiliar sounds, sprinted from the wheat field to a nearby forest. For the wildlife, their habitat no longer resembled the pastoral hills and fields they were accustomed to visiting.

    Invading forces of the Union Army of the Potomac and the Confederate Army of Northern Virginia jockeyed for the best position on the hills and farmland surrounding the town of Gettysburg, Pennsylvania. An eerie silence followed the cannonade as the Southern artillery reloaded their weapons to soften up the Union defenses along Cemetery Ridge.

    "Willie! Stay down! Keep low!" Alex McPhail yelled to his comrade who clung to the grassy mound three feet from him.

    For the first time in two years, Alex saw fear in Willie's eyes. She cried out to him, "I'm scared. I don't want either of us to die. We've been through too much together."

    Seconds later, Alex heard the hiss of the cannon ball as it sliced through the air. Then came the scream—from the woman beside him whose secret kept her fighting for the Union since the war began. The impact of the leaden ball shattered Willie's knee sending shards of bone through her slender thigh, followed by streams of blood.

For a moment, Alex stared in disbelief. Then his adrenaline kicked in and he crawled to Willie's side as she slipped into unconsciousness. *Dear God don't let her die. We belong together. She's mine. You can't take her.* He stroked her flushed face with trembling fingers then followed the line of her chin to her throat where he located the pulse. It grew fainter with each beat of her heart. Tears stung his eyes. There was nothing he could do for her.

General Meade commanded his troops. "Take up your positions. Pickett's decided to charge. We're right in their crosshairs. Give it all you've got, boys. Sound the bugles and forward march."

Alex hesitated and began to drag Willie out of the pathway of trampling feet and moving artillery when his commander pointed at him and shouted, "You, by the fallen lad, move. The ambulance wagon is behind and will get him if he's still alive. On your feet—that's an order."

With a heavy heart, anger stirred in Alex's belly. He grabbed his musket, took one last glance at Willie and charged toward the enemy.

Chapter Two

Dwindling daylight ushered in evening shadows with blessed relief to those who survived the day's battles. Weary Union soldiers held their own territory and forced General Lee's army to retreat. A thread of jubilant victory ran through the ranks but the only satisfaction Alex felt was the opportunity to avenge the attack on Willie. Several artillery men took their last breath because of his accurate aim.

Men, tired and hungry, made their way back to the bivouac and flopped down beside their tent. No sooner had Alex secured his musket inside his shelter when Hans, Willie's twin brother, appeared, barely recognizable with dirt, blood and exhaustion covering his whisker-stubbled face. His eyes scanned the immediate area, then he lifted the flap to Willie's tent. Empty. Panic forced him to cry out, "Where is she? She promised she'd always stay close to either one of us." Hans grabbed Alex by the shoulders and shook him. "Tell me she's still alive."

Alex lifted his head as tears streamed down his gritty face, and looked into his friend's anxious eyes. For a moment, he couldn't say the words and Hans shook harder. In a trembling voice, Alex told him the events of the afternoon. By the time he finished, both men were sobbing as each cradled the other.

"We've got to find her. I can't leave my sister out there among the dead. Get your lantern. I'll search all night if I have to."

While lighting the wick, Alex remembered the words of his commander, *an ambulance is not far behind*. A ray of hope surfaced from within his battered emotions.

"Hans, wait. We'll check the infirmary first."

On their arrival, the smell of blood, mutilated flesh, feces and urine filled their nostrils where wounded men moaned and cried. Frazzled surgeons hurried from one patient to another with vials of morphine to ease their pain. Piles of amputated limbs stacked outside the tent contributed to the growing stench.

An army nurse watched Alex and Hans walk the narrow pathways between the cots as they looked in vain for the woman they both loved. Finally, he stepped toward Alex and asked, "What's his name?"

Hans spoke up, "Willie Baden. My twin brother—a little smaller than me. Hit in the leg by a cannon ball."

The nurse stared at the stranger with the dimpled cheek before asking, "Take off your hat, sir. Let me see your hair color."

Hans obliged, running his hand through sweat-soaked tousled strands of blond curls.

Alex saw the expression change on the man's face from one of indifference to genuine concern as once more he looked at Hans's countenance.

"The ambulance brought in someone who fits the description of the injury and as I look at you," he paused, "there is a resemblance but it wasn't a male."

Both men looked at each other and held their breath. Each read the other's thoughts. *If she came to the infirmary with a crushed leg, the surgeons and nurse would know upon examination she was a woman.*

"Could it be your sister?"

"Yes, sir."

"Poor soul," muttered the nurse. "We had to amputate her leg from the knee down."

Alex heard a guttural moan gurgle up from within Hans and in an instant his own stomach turned nauseous as he pictured the procedure. But once again, hope sprang from within his grief. *She's alive. How could I doubt her will to live?*

"Hans, Willie is alive."

***

CONVICTIONS

An occasional burst of sparks flared up from the campfire into the jeweled night sky. Bacon crackled in the iron skillet. Normally, Alex and Hans devoured this daily fare, but not this evening. A sickly sensation replaced the hunger pangs.

"Here," urged Alex as he withdrew strips of pork from the red-hot skillet and handed a plate to Hans. "I'm not hungry either, but we have to eat. There's a couple pieces of hardtack in my sack we can fry in the grease."

"It's my fault." Hans said as he took the meager ration. "Why did I ever believe she could disguise herself as a man and fight in this hell? But then..." Hans hesitated before he continued, "we didn't see things as they really are. Romantic fools thinking the war would be over in a few months. Two years later and we're still dodging bullets. Mighty lucky to be alive after Fredericksburg. Should have sent her home."

Alex spoke the truth. "She wouldn't have gone. You know that as well as I do. My feelings for your sister run deep, friend. She touched my heart like no other woman. We'll find her, Hans. As Mammy told me time after time, 'God always has a plan.'" *As sure as I take my next breath, I'll never forget you, Winona Baden.*

***

Flickering light from the flame of a single candle caught Winona's attention as her eyes opened. *Where am I?* She looked around the small spartan room. *Back in the orphanage? And who is wiping my face?* She tried to speak but only a weak whisper came out. "Water."

Instantly, Winona heard the lady in the white head covering and black robe call to her companion, "She's coming round. Praise be to God. Our prayers have been answered, Sister. Help me lift her up so she can swallow."

Winona felt strong arms raise her body to a sitting position as one of the nuns pressed a tin cup, full of cool water, against her burning lips. "Drink, dear, your body needs liquids."

Gulping the needed nourishment, Winona's eyes surveyed

first one woman and then the other. She noted both were dressed alike. They even wore the same genial expression on their faces. *Am I in a convent?*

The elder nun saw confusion on Winona's face and as she refilled the cup explained, "My name is Sister Mary and this is Sister Francis. Our home is called Sisters of Mercy. The hospital filled after the battle, so they brought you to us."

A frown crossed Winona's forehead. *Battle? What battle?*

Sister Francis, anxious to cut in continued, "You've been delirious with fever for three days." She raised her rosary to her lips. "We've prayed for you every hour."

No sooner did Winona utter the word, "Th-an-k..." when she winced. It felt as though a hot blade seared the skin the full length of her left leg. She reached down to sooth her shin and felt ragged edges of a bandage that covered her stub. Trembling fingers groped further—nothing. Fear knotted inside her stomach and disbelief drained her face of color as she screamed, "My leg is gone! Why?" Shock raged through her body and she began to shake uncontrollably.

Winona felt Sister Mary's arms wrap around her upper body and hold her close as though she were comforting a child. It took several minutes for the initial trauma of amputation to register in her mind and her sobbing gasps finally gave way to a whimper. Streams of salty tears continued to flow down her face like a never-ending spring soaking the front of her cotton nightdress.

Sister Francis pulled a clean, white linen handkerchief from the folds of her tunic, handed it to her, and tried to console. "You are not the first, Willie, to lose a limb in this terrible war. So many soldiers return home missing an arm or a leg. We'll help you learn to adjust."

Winona snapped back, "How could I lose part of my leg in a war? I'm a woman. Women don't fight battles. And my name is Winona, not Willie." Another round of tears erupted. "Leave me alone. I need to think. Nothing makes any sense. Maybe I'm losing my mind."

As the two nuns closed the door, they took another look at

their patient and made the sign of the cross. In the hallway, Sister Mary spoke the truth.

"I fear, Sister, that not only will we need to pray for Winona's physical healing, but healing of another sort—amnesia. She's put the battle at Gettysburg out of her memory."

Chapter Three

Two years earlier, 1861

Thunder boomed. Lightening flashed. A gust of wind sent a weak live oak branch crashing against the dining room window. Inside the mansion, another storm simmered. One with the potential to change the course of an eighteen year-old's life.

Searing parental words lashed out at Alex McPhail.

"I'll disown you. No son of Angus McPhail shall be called a traitor!" A creeping flush of redness worked its way up a burgeoning neck and settled beneath strands of a whitening beard. In an instant, a clenched fist slammed into the oak table rattling the fine china. The tirade continued, "Secession was inevitable. The South can go it alone. Cotton is king and tobacco is just as profitable. We have the climate and the work force to produce exports as lucrative as anything the northern states can manufacture in their industrialized factories. We're not dependant on the crumbs that drop from the Union's table."

"But father, Grandfather fought in the Revolutionary War to help establish a free united Republic. I sat on your lap as a child and heard you tell me stories of grandfather's struggle and his fight for freedom. Over and over you told us how he escaped as a bond servant from the English tyranny in Scotland. Did he not risk his life when he boarded a ship as a stow-away to come to America to start a new life?" Alex took a calming breath before continuing, "If you don't believe in the Republic, then tell me why you voted in favor of Florida's statehood, a mere sixteen years ago?

"I'll tell you why." Angus, stood, his six-foot frame towered over Alex and he pointed a finger at his son. "When I heard the Territory of Florida offered free land to those who would come here and settle, I packed my belongings, left Boston, and headed south. Like my father who saw America as the land of opportunity, I visualized the soil you live on as my chance to advance in life. Here in Tallahassee, the farmland is rich. Bales of cotton picked from our own fields are hauled to ships and exported around the world." Another clash of thunder threatened to drown out the words of pride spewing from Angus's lips.

Alex braced himself for a lengthy speech—much of which he'd heard before but he knew better than to get up and leave. Angus McPhail did not believe in sparing the rod.

His father continued, "The demand for cotton soon outgrew our acreage and a group of us realized the only way to increase the size of our properties was to apply for statehood. Then we could buy land from the government. Money for improvements and railway service soon followed. At last, Florida had a representative in the federal government."

Alex contained himself no longer. The nerves in his stomach twitched and the saliva in his mouth dried up leaving a parchness that made it difficult to speak as he confronted the man whose ruddy image he bore. Perspiration beaded on his tanned forehead and slowly trickled down chiseled cheekbones. "So you used the Republic to further your wealth and now you're casting it aside? That's wrong. You'll regret it someday, Father."

Cold, unyielding eyes locked into Alex's and despite the sweltering humidity in the room, a shiver raced through the young man's slender, developing body.

"How dare you question your father's integrity? Who's planting these blasphemous ideas in your head? Surely it isn't the expensive military school you've been privileged to attend. If so, I can put a stop to that, lad."

Unable to sit any longer, Alex rose, pushed his chair under the table, and grasped the carved frame to steady his weakening knees until his knuckles turned white. *I refuse to be intimidated. This confrontation has been a long time coming and I'll not walk away like a beaten dog.* Without the bat of an eyelash, he forged ahead.

"Am I not allowed to speak my own mind in this house? You have sixty slaves who do your bidding—no voice of their own. Is that not enough for you?" Alex heard the deep intake of his father's breath, ready to explode in a torrent of words but it did not stop him. He stretched out his right arm and yanked at the shirt material until it exposed naked flesh. "Look Father." Each word grew louder by decibels. "Do you see black skin or white? I'm not one of them. I have a voice and if you won't listen, I'll find others who will."

"And you'll not inherit one inch of this property. Oak Haven will go solely to your sister." A moment of silence passed, eyes locked, as each processed the deep meaning intended to break Alex's spirit.

"Then so be it, sir."

Angus McPhail watched speechless as his son turned sharply and walked out into the rain.

Chapter Four

One last deluge of rain drenched Alex from his wavy auburn hair down to the soles of his boots. Afternoon storms in Florida were common but getting wet was the least of his worries. While his father's biting words were still fresh in his mind, his thoughts waffled. *Perhaps I should have bit my tongue. Kept my opinion to myself—surrendered to his politics.* Determination took the upper hand and once again a strange new strength summoned him to admit. *If I give in, I'll never be the man my grandfather would want me to be. Now is the hour. Now is the time.*

Alex stopped and looked around at the surrounding acreage. Live oak branches, laden with Spanish moss, formed a canopy over the brick roadway leading up to the main two-story house on the one- thousand acre plantation. Three front columns stood like sentinels as they supported the roof of a wrap-around porch. At the pinnacle of the structure, a widow's walk offered a spectacular view of the surrounding cotton fields. Behind the stone 'big house', a sandy, well-trodden trail led down an incline through a stand of pine and oak until it stopped at an open area known as the 'quarters'. Whitewashed wooden cabins, six feet apart, formed a horseshoe-shaped community wherein dwelled slaves bought and sold by Angus McPhail.

He knocked at the door of cabin three, it opened and a strapping young man with beads of water glistening among sprigs of black, tightly- wound hair took his arm and pulled him inside.

"Alex, what you doin' out in the storm? I almost got soaked myself runnin' from the cotton shed." He shook his head and a spray of water flew off.

"I had to get away from him, Joshua."

"What this time?"

"Can't tell you here. Someone might hear. I reckon the storm's past so come with me to our favorite oak tree." Alex looked around the barren room. The simplicity of it always gnawed at his conscience—a table with two benches, a fireplace, a lantern, and straw mats for sleeping. He had so much; they had so little. Yet, from the time he was a child, he felt safe here. "Where's your mammy?"

"She up at the big house. Don't you 'member your sister, Mary Ellen get married tomorrow? Mammy workin' hard to prepare food for the party."

Alex threw his hands in the air. "How could I forget? That's all she's talked about for weeks."

"C'mon, let's go 'fore Mammy gets back. You go first like we always do. Then I follows. Ain't nobody after all these years bin able to find us." Joshua snickered. "We's good."

A streak of sunlight brightened the sky as a breeze blew the clouds farther east. Alex looked around to be sure he wasn't being followed then headed into the woods. A quarter mile from the quarters, alongside a creek, an ancient live oak spread thick branches from bottom to top. Perfect for climbing. In seconds, Alex shimmied ten feet up its trunk, then sat and waited for his friend. For years, they'd shared secrets, joys, sorrows, fears and mischief sitting in this hallowed place.

Presently, Alex heard Joshua humming a tune as he strutted up to the tree and began his climb. Curious, Alex asked, "You ever come here when I'm away at school?"

"Not like we used to. Ain't the same by myself. Except for once." Joshua's face grew solemn and he bent his head. For a few seconds, only the sound of a bird broke the silence.

"And what happened," urged Alex.

Joshua swung his bare feet then pulled up his right leg and traced a six-inch scar on his calf. "That's where the whip slashed me. I 'bout bit my tongue off to keep quiet. Wouldn't give him no satisfaction."

"Who did it? And why?" Anger stirred in Alex's stomach.

Joshua hesitated and hung his head again.

"Tell me." Alex's determination broke his friend's silence.

"Your daddy." Joshua heard the sudden intake of breath and saw his friend's reddening cheeks and distraught eyes.

"What'd you do?"

"Nothin'. It weren't me who stole his whiskey. He kept it in the root cellar and when he came lookin' for it, I was gettin' taters for Mammy to cook for his supper. Told me I was lyin' and never to set foot in there again. Took me outside, grabbed a whip from his buggy, and set about to teach me a lesson. Later that night, I sees ole Simon passin' the bottle around to his friends. I hates to say it, Alex, but you got a mean father and we's got a mean massa."

Alex nodded. "That's what I want to tell you. We argued about secession today and I know if he'd had a whip close by, I'd be nursing my wounds. Told me if I didn't stop talking about how wrong it is to separate from the Union he'd disown me—give everything to Mary Ellen. I told him to do just that, then walked away."

Joshua turned toward Alex so quickly he almost fell out of the tree. "You crazy, man. This plantation yours when massa dies. We your property, too. What your sister know about runnin' this place?"

"Listen, Joshua, it's not right that you're a slave. We're supposed to be equal. Since we were born, you one week before me, we've been close as brothers. When my mother died giving birth to me, it was your mammy who raised me. We both sucked our milk from the same breast. I taught you to read, write and do sums. From the time we could walk, we felt the warm soil between our toes. Remember how we chased each other from one end of this plantation to the other? Don't you want more for your life than pickin' cotton?"

"Course I do but it ain't gonna change."

"Alex took a deep breath and asked, "Joshua, have you been reading that Bible I gave you?"

"Sure 'nough. I reads to Mammy. She mighty proud."

"Do you remember reading about the Hebrew slaves in Egypt?" Joshua nodded. "You think they didn't feel the same as you? Thought they were stuck forever. But God didn't forget them, did he?"

Joshua's face brightened and his lips curled around white, even teeth as he spoke, "Brought them out of there and took them into a new land where they was free. You hear us sing about that some nights around the fire. Mammy told me she picked my name from that story. She tell me to grow up strong and help my people like that other Joshua done."

"Listen, it won't be easy. In fact, I overheard some leaders at my academy one evening talkin'. I was on after dinner clean-up duty and one of the Lieutenants come right out and said there was going to be a war against the Union."

The whites of Joshua's eyes grew big as a full moon. "You sure you hear that right?"

"Sure as I'm sitting here. Somethin' 'bout President Lincoln sending troops to a fort in South Carolina. The new Confederacy is afraid the Union will force the slave states back into the Republic and set y'all free."

"Your daddy not like that. Noo— siree. You scared?"

Alex brushed a lock of crimped hair out of his vision and stared straight ahead before answering. "Since I heard that news I've been doing a powerful lot of thinkin'."

"What 'bout? How to fight?"

Alex chuckled and gave his friend a good-natured jab in the ribs. "You know I can fight. We've been wrestling and lickin' each other since the day Mammy took a switch to our behinds to get us to stop."

"Never did no good though," Joshua bragged as a smile replaced the concern on his face. "We just got better."

"I reckon. Besides, for the past two years the military school taught me how to be a proper soldier. I'm not afraid to fight, Josh." Alex took a deep breath and slowly exhaled. "My problem is I'm not sure yet what side I want to fight on."

Chapter Five

Sue Ellen awoke from a deep sleep as rays of welcomed sunshine flooded the bedroom and beckoned her to throw off the coverings from the comfortable feather bed. She stretched her slender arms above a thick mass of braided red hair, tinted with gold streaks, and smiled. A silent prayer followed as she slipped to the floor, tip-toed to the window and pulled up the sash. A refreshing April breeze tickled the soft, freckled skin on her face. *Thank you, Lord, the storm is gone and you've given me a perfect day for my garden wedding.*

Directly below, sounds of clanging skillets, tingling glasses and silver eating utensils signaled breakfast preparation. The enticing aroma of rich, freshly ground coffee mingled with the fried bacon wafting up to the second floor were enough to start Sue Ellen's stomach growling. She hadn't eaten much at last night's dinner. She concluded it was simply a matter of wedding preparation jitters but she also felt a nagging tension hovering over the entire meal. *I wonder why Alex barely spoke. That's not like my brother with his out-spoken opinions. There was no eye contact between him and Father either. Thank goodness Andrew and his parents were our guests. I feel so blessed to have a fiancé with a sense of humor. Oh, well, I guess this spat will blow over like all the rest.*

By the time Sue Ellen descended the winding staircase to the dining room, Mammy was in a tither. Her brown brow glistened with perspiration and she wiped her pudgy hands over and over on her worn apron.

"Lawdy, lawdy, Missy, what you 'bin doin'? You forgets this

yor weddin' day? I's got food layin' all over the kitchen waitin' for yor blessin'. I don't wants no guest goin' home sayin' I can't cooks. "Sides, we gots to get you bathed, hair washed,

and dressed in that perdy gown. Now hurry cause time's a-wastin'. 'For we knows it, the preacher will be here at noon and you still in your nightdress."

Sue Ellen smiled at the one woman on this plantation she loved the most. Mammy's arms had cradled her from the time she was five-years old, wiped her tears when she ran into a swarm of bees, taught her how to cook, and prepared her for marriage. *Life without a mother would have been unbearable if it hadn't been for this dear soul.*

Sue Ellen gulped a cup of warm coffee, grabbed a corn muffin, and headed for the kitchen. A menu of fried chicken, ham, turkey, sweet potatoes, coleslaw, deviled eggs, fruit, cakes, and an assortment of breads filled every inch of counter space. By the time she sampled each platter, she could not swallow another bite.

"No need to worry, Mammy, they'll be coming back for seconds."

***

As the clock ticked on, Sue Ellen felt butterflies tickle her tummy. There was no doubt in her mind this day would change her life forever. No longer would her father be the center of her world but a man she fell in love with two years ago at a church social. Not interested in growing cotton, Andrew chose to spread the gospel among those who attended the growing congregation at First Presbyterian Church near Tallahassee. Sue Ellen felt she was ready to be a pastor's wife. She'd studied her bible, memorized the verses, and sang not only songs from the hymnal but spirituals Mammy sang to her as smooth, black arms cuddled and rocked her to sleep.

Finally, after much primping, Sue Ellen, was ready to say her vows under the garden arbor where Confederate Jasmine filled the air with a natural breath-taking scent sweeter than any perfume. She saw tears slide down Angus's cheeks the moment his eyes saw his daughter descend the oak stairway dressed in an exquisite ivory taffeta, hoop-skirt gown. Fine lace ran along the edge of the sweetheart neckline and down the sleeves to the ruffled cuffs. Above the hemline, appliquéd orange blossoms adorned yards of scalloped silk.

Taking Sue Ellen's arm, Angus bent down and whispered, "You're the image of your mother. I so wish she could be here to see what a lovely lady you've become."

Not used to compliments from her father, she blushed and her cheeks turned a delicate pink. "Come Father; I don't want Andrew thinking I've changed my mind."

While guests sat on satin covered chairs waiting for the bride to appear, they listened to the soft mellow notes of a harp. Alex, dressed in a starched white shirt, grey waistcoat and trousers, served as an usher. His good looks caught the eye of every young girl as they vied to take his arm and follow him to their seat. One staked her claim to him immediately.

Bella Daniels batted her long, black eye-lashes, squeezed his arm and in a velvet voice said, "I'll be waiting for you on our favorite swing under the sycamore. Bring a lemonade, pl-e-a-se." Bella's beguiling smile set Alex's pulse racing.

The wedding, short, but meaningful brought the house servants to the windows to peek out at a ceremony that was denied to a slave.

"Where the broom, Mammy?" asked a young man.

"Ain't no broom. White folk don't jump no broom. We's the only ones do."

"Then who gonna be the boss in da family? Whoever jump the highest is the one who give da orders." A snicker followed. "I be practicin' mighty hard before I finds me a wife."

A round of laughter from the other servants was interrupted by cheers and congratulations as the guests hugged and shook hands with the newly-married couple. Out of the shadows came platters of food, drink and confectionaries. With appetites satisfied, the afternoon soon turned to games, relaxation, and talk.

On his way to meet Bella, Alex with her drink in hand, slowed his pace as he approached a group of men huddled together beneath the shade of an oak tree. One of the gentlemen announced, "The war won't last three days".

Alex stopped, his ears tuned in on every word and he listened with intent.

"If President Lincoln thinks he can intimidate the southern states by sending more troops to Fort Sumpter then I say we need to call his bluff," expressed another elderly gentleman stomping the ground with his cane. "Show 'em we southern folk know how to fight." A shout of triumph pierced the air as each man raised a clenched fist. "Seems the Republic has forgotten Andrew Jackson at the Battle of New Orleans. Sent those British a-runnin' we did."

"All this talk of unity among the states is hogwash," added another. "We have nothin' in common with the Union anymore. We got the climate, the labor, cotton and tobacco to fuel the economy. The south needs to send Lincoln a message—leave us alone."

Conflicting thoughts darted about in Alex's head and he almost blurted out that caste systems in his opinion are wrong. Keeping a segment of the population ignorant and dependent does not grow economies. But he remained silent. He knew no one in this group was sympathetic to his views and he didn't want to incite his father's wrath on Sue Ellen's wedding day. Instead, he looked for Bella. He knew he was late and her ire was all he cared to handle.

True to form, she sat straight in the swing, her dainty chin turned up in agitation. "Well, did you have to squeeze the lemons and make the lemonade yourself? I've been waiting for over half an hour. After all, I am a guest, Alex."

"And a mighty pretty one, too." Having known Bella for a few years, Alex knew her weak spot. "Is that a new hair style? Those curls make you look so mature."

A weakening smile broke the girl's icy countenance and she motioned for him to sit beside her. "So what were you doing?"

"Listening in on politics. Nothing that would interest you. Although, it probably will affect you."

A shadow of a pout crossed her dimpled face. "How so?"

Alex took her right hand in his and looked into naive eyes before explaining,

"I believe the states that seceded are going to war against the North. Some say that President Lincoln wants to fight and if it lasts for many months our way of life will change."

"But darlin', you'll still be here won't you?" Bella feigned wiping a tear from her eye. "I can't bear the thought of you going to war."

Alex squeezed her hand. "Let's not talk about it now. Look, over there by the water fountain. Our friends are playing croquette. Come. Let's join them." Alex pulled her off the swing and together they walked hand in hand.

***

By early evening the bride and groom changed into traveling clothes and mingled for a short time among the guests. Andrew and Sue Ellen expressed their gratitude to each person for coming and making it a perfect day. Alex, tired of placating Bella, slipped away and waited by the decorated carriage. It was laden with luggage, ready to transport the newlyweds to Tallahassee where they intended to catch the train to St. Augustine. As he drew his sister into an affectionate embrace, he whispered into her ear, "I need to talk to you when you return."

Sue Ellen drew back and gave Alex a quizzical look. "Sounds serious. Now you have tweaked my curiosity and I'll have it on my mind the whole time I'm away. Blast you, brother." She slapped her silken glove against his cheek.

Alex's diaphragm shook with laughter and he looked in Andrew's direction. "Somehow I believe my new brother-in-law will center your thoughts on him—not Oak Haven. At least I surely hope so. Bye, sis, I love you."

Chapter Six

April 13, 1861, the morning after Sue Ellen's wedding, Oak Haven resumed normal activities. Slaves, in the fields since sun-up, hitched the plows and guided the horses and mules up and down the black, fertile soil cutting a furrow in the softened earth. Behind them came the planters, each with a sack full of cotton seed strung across their chest weighing down hunched shoulders. Careful not to spill or deposit the sacred content in other than the intended trench, not an eye dared to wander or this action resulted in a lash of the whip from the overseer.

Up at the 'big house', Mammy prepared to do the day's laundry. Out behind a wash shed, a circular area, three feet across and one foot deep, surrounded by bricks, held chopped hunks of firewood that provided the fire to heat water in a copper tub. A cake of lye soap bobbed up and down as the liquid began to boil.

Alex smelled the smoke from his window and looked down to see Mammy deposit shirts into the frenzied water, then take a wooden paddle and swirl them around and around the tub. He quickly dressed, picked up his soiled clothes from yesterday, raced down the stairs, and out the back door.

"Mornin' Mammy. Brought you another batch. Sorry I didn't bring 'em sooner. Guess I slept in."

Mammy glanced up at the rising sun and exclaimed, " 'Shornuf." That what happen when you out spooin' with that gal from yonder plantation last night. Why Joshua done plant half an acre by now."

Alex wasn't sure if the look on her face was a tease or a scold so he changed the subject. "Father around?" The nerves in his stomach tightened.

"No he ain't. Had him an early breakfast and went into town."

Alex exhaled relief. He and Angus hadn't spoken in two days.

Mammy looked at Alex. " Supose you hungry now." She lay down the paddle and started toward the kitchen. "Come on. I gots fresh cornbread and grits waitin' for ya. These here clothes gots to stew awhiles."

Rather than sit alone in the elegant dining room, Alex preferred the casual comfort of pulling up a chair to the hewn pine kitchen table. He especially enjoyed watching Mammy knead the rising dough that within hours would transform into mouth-watering biscuits.

"Seems strange without Sue Ellen around, doesn't it?" he said.

"You know your sister and Andrew gonna live with us 'till the parsonage built over by the church, don't cha? Your daddy insists. He tells me to prepare their room 'fore they gets back. The one with the sittin' room and big windows. Used to be your mamas'." Mammy's voice softened and the room went quiet.

Alex spooned the remaining grits together in his bowl before asking a question that had been on his mind for some time.

"Mammy, where's Josh's daddy? Why isn't he here at Oak Haven?"

Taken by surprise, her flour-covered fingers stopped kneading and Mammy's face took on a peculiar look–almost fear. She wiped her hands on her apron, and turned away before answering. "He gone. Your daddy sold him when Joshua born. It happen to many black slave womans."

Alex swallowed the grits and in a burst of emotion shouted, "But why? That's so cruel."

Mammy wiped a tear from her watering eyes with the corner of her apron, sniffed a couple of times and explained, "Slaves not allowed to have a legal wedding cause then massers can separate man and woman and not feel like they's split up a family."

"Does Josh know what happened to his father?"

"Yes, I tell him a few years ago. He say he don't ever want to be separated from a woman he love so he not even lookin' for one." Mammy sighed. "I prays every night to the Lawd that my baby don't get sold and takin' away from me."

Alex got up from the table, walked over to Mammy, smiled then squeezed her shoulder. "Don't worry. Not if I have anything to say about it." Changing the subject he announced, "My horse needs exercise; I'll be out for a while."

***

The smell of hay and manure awakened the senses in Alex's nostrils and lead him in the direction of the horse stable. Barney, the blacksmith, withdrew a glowing-red iron rod from the smoldering forge that stood outside the building and placed it on an anvil. Without delay and with expert precision, the black man picked up a hammer and began to mold the iron rod into a U-shape. To complete the task, he plunged the hot iron into a bucket of cold water. Hissing steam immediately filled the air. Finally cooled, a new horseshoe was ready to protect the feet of one of the work horses needed to farm cotton.

Alex admired the strength and bulging muscles on this man's glistening upper arms as the hammer came down with a clang and struck the soften metal over and over.

"A fine job you're doing, Barney. No one can make a shoe as good as you. Our horses are the better for your work."

Barney smiled. "Thank you, Masser Alex." Sweat dripped off the tip of his nose and sizzled as each drop hit the iron. "Your horse gots new shoes yesterday. Did it myself cause I know you like it done gentle like."

"That I do. Animals have feelin's just like us humans. I know you understand, don't you?"

Barney nodded before answering, "Yes, sir, I sure 'nouf do."

Alex caught the inference behind the blacksmith's response and veered the conversation in another direction.

"I believe my horse is the best looking steed on Oak Haven. If anyone comes lookin' for me tell 'em Starlight and I are out in the fields."

Alex guided his quarter horse away from the out-buildings and into the acres of open space. The fresh spring air felt intoxicating. Even Starlight's gait was light and energized. As horse and rider trampled the earth, the smell of moist, rich soil not yet arid from a blazing summer sun, added to the rebirth of a season.

A familiar sight drew Alex's attention as he neared long furrows of tilled land. A procession of slaves, men, women, and young children slowly went through the same routine —one hand reached into a bag, extracted cotton seed and dropped it into the soil while the other helped balance the load. They repeated this process while an overseer, with a bull-whip in hand, sat on his horse behind them observing the progress. Should he not be satisfied, one snap of the raw hide sent fear rippling down the line and quickened the planting.

Crack! Alex's ears perked up at the repulsive sound and his eyes scanned the field for its source. Several yards near the end of a furrow he spotted Jenkins, his right hand thrashing a snake-like whip in the air, ready to strike a victim. Adrenaline surged through Alex and he prodded Starlight into a gallop toward the scene. On the ground, lay an elderly man, his white frizzled hair saturated in blood from an oozing scalp wound. Cotton seed spilled from his sack and scattered in all directions.

Darts of anger shot from the overseer's cold, black eyes as the muscles on his weathered face twitched causing a pencil-thin moustache to move like a slithering snake. "Pick 'em up! Every last one or you'll feel another sting across your back."

Jenkins raised his right hand poised to strike again but before he could, Alex rode up from behind, halted Starlight, pulled his Colt revolver out of its sheath and commanded, "One more lash and you're a dead man."

Caught by surprise, Jenkins turned in his saddle to look down the barrel of Alex's gun. "You don't have the nerve, fancy nigger lover. Just 'cause you bin to military school don't mean nothin'."

The surrounding slaves stopped their work and stood mesmerized. Alex continued to stand his ground. This time he cocked the weapon and took aim. Not once did his eyes leave Jenkins's face.

"Your father will hear about this. I'm under his orders, not yours."

"And if you don't throw down the whip and leave this man, it won't be you, telling this tale, Jenkins"

A hard stare between the two, resulted in the overseer releasing the whip and spurring his horse forward, barely missing the injured slave as he galloped down the corridor between the rows.

Chapter Seven

Angus bounded up the steps to the 'big house' yelling and waving a newspaper. The ruddiness in his face deepening. "It's war! We're at war with the North. Finally we Southerners are ready to put Lincoln in his place."

The unexpected commotion brought Mammy scurrying from the kitchen clenching a rolling pin. Seconds later, Alex hurried down the stairway into the foyer where they both came face-to-face with Angus.

"Calm down, Father," urged Alex. "What's this about war?"

Angus took a deep breath and began again. "Early this morning, at 4:30 a.m., General Beauregard ordered the first cannon to fire on Fort Sumter in Charleston Harbor. Major Robert Anderson evacuated the fort at noon today." He raised a triumphant fist in the air.

Alex felt his stomach quiver as he tried to digest the words predicted by his military instructor one month ago. *So the time has come. The fabric of our nation is to be torn from north to south.* A bitter taste in his mouth preceded the bile he forced to swallow.

A look of bewilderment crossed Mammy's face and she blurted, "What this mean, Masser? Who gonna fight? You? Alex? My people?"

Angus placed a hand on Mammy's arm to quiet her concern. "Your people will stay at Oak Haven and carry on as usual. Nothing's going to change."

Alex, still stunned at the news, remained silent but thought differently. *Nothing will be the same, Father. All the rumors of* war with the North have come true. What if the South is not prepared to take this bold action?

An avalanche of questions filled his mind but one certainty he knew. Within a few days he would be forced to make the biggest decision of his life.

***

By seven o'clock that evening, Angus's library smelled of Cuban cigars. Smoke wafted idly from chair to chair and glasses filled with Scotch whiskey clinked together as Angus and his business friends offered a toast to the Confederacy. Cheers followed.

The general assumption among the men was that Lincoln, in a covert fashion, wanted the South to strike first. Edgar Collins, owner of the neighboring plantation, offered his opinion. "Consider the facts, gentlemen. Lincoln spurned our Confederate efforts to settle differences with the Union."

A chorus of agreement encouraged Mr. Collins to continue. "South Carolina could hardly be expected to tolerate Union forces at Fort Sumter—right in the middle of the harbor. I believe Lincoln knew that would be a thorn not tolerated and sooner or later Confederates would fire the first cannon."

Heads nodded through the maze of smoke. Another man added his thoughts.

"He may have hoped this action would inspire other states who have not yet seceded to join forces to restore the Union."

"Time will tell, but in the meantime, we need to think smartly," urged Angus. "Wars may be fought over many things but one fact always remains. Somebody has to supply the soldiers with food, guns, clothing—the list goes on and on. There's money to be made, gentlemen. Most of us are too old to fight but we know how to grow our wealth."

Alex heard every word as he sat near the door pretending to read. To think his father was willing to use war as a means to profit sickened his stomach and he got up and walked out into the refreshing coolness of the night. As he leaned against the porch railing, a harmonious melody filtered up through the pines and oak trees from the quarters. The slaves often gathered around a bonfire and sang. Songs of freedom and inspirational hymns kept their spirits alive with hope for a better future.

In his heart, Alex knew this group of people who had watched him reach manhood, influenced the impending decision that hung over his head like the sword of Damocles. As the singing waned and the embers from the fire grew cold, he felt a peace in his heart and he walked to his room to make plans.

Chapter Eight

"Alex, get up, we need to talk." Angus clenched his fist and pounded twice on his son's bedroom door. No response. "Answer me." The pounding continued.

Awakened by the sound of his father's voice, Alex threw back the covers, jumped from his bed, and opened the door. "What's wrong? I was sleeping."

Angus stretched out his right hand and poked his son in the chest with his forefinger. The muscles in his face tightened and his eyes focused on Alex's questioning expression. "Who's the master of Oak Haven?" He waited.

"You...are, sir," stammered Alex. *Where is he going with this?* The answer came to him. *Aw, Jenkins made good on his threat.*

"Who gave you the authority to pull a gun on my overseer yesterday? The man was doing his job?"

No longer in a sleep-like state, Alex was quick with his defense. "Hired to oversee that the planting is done properly or hired to whip an old man who stumbled? Amos is too old to work the fields. Blood ran from his head until he could no longer stand. Working our slaves 'til they keel over is not productive. Why can't we treat ours like other plantation owners? Get rid of Jenkins, Father. He's giving Oak Haven a bad reputation."

Alex saw the throbbing vein that ran up the side of Angus's neck and knew they were on a collision course.

"Watch your sass, young man. You got your mama's way of thinkin'—weak, vulnerable. You need to be strong— in control. You can't let slaves get the upper hand. I'm leaving for Atlanta this morning. I'll be gone four or five days. With the war getting started, there'll be a need for pork and I intend to be one of the first to supply our men. I need good breeders, fast turnover and hefty hogs. By the time I get back, Oak Haven will be raising more than cotton." Angus gave Alex a stern look. "Try to stay out of trouble. I'm warning you. Jenkins is now your enemy. I'd watch my back if I were you."

Alex pursed his lips and nodded. Every nerve in Alex's body fought to keep calm. *Lord, help me. Don't let me strike my own father.*

Angus turned to leave, paused, then looked at his son. "There's a militia organizing in town. When I return, I expect to see you dressed in uniform ready to drill." The sound of his heavy footsteps echoed down the stairs and drifted into the distance.

***

Mammy recognized the look. She'd seen despair on Alex's face every time he and his father had a dispute. Her large bosom swelled then fell as she exhaled a sigh. *What dis time, chile? When you and your daddy ever gonna agree on anything?* She placed a bowl of steaming grits in front of Alex as he took a seat at the table. He said nothing but picked up a spoon and stirred the contents as he waited for them to cool.

Mammy watched out of the corner of her eye. She saw Alex fidget, the muscles around his mouth twitched as though he tried to speak. Finally the words gushed from his tightened lips. "I'm leaving, Mammy. I can't stay any longer."

Mammy dropped the can of lard she held and looked straight at her young charge. Her knees went weak and she sat on the bench beside him. "What you mean, leavin'? Where you go?"

"I won't fight in a Confederate army. If I don't leave soon, Father will have me signed up and I'll be trapped. I'm going to town and wire Uncle Robert in Boston to tell him I'm on my way."

"You want to join the Union army?" Tears rolled one after the other down the dark, plump cheeks of this servant until they splashed onto her apron.

"If they'll have me. You, of all folks, understand why I have to do it, don't you, Mammy?"

Tender hands squeezed Alex's arm and she nodded. "I hates to see you go but 'course I do. No one know your daddy better than I. You not at all like him; you sweet and gentle, but strong too." Mammy's voice trembled as she continued, "Joshua gonna miss you. You two like brothers. Not on the outside, mind ya," she grinned, "but on the inside where it count."

Alex replied, "Let me be the one to tell him what I plan to do. I need his help."

Mammy wiped her eyes, stood, and placed a comforting hand on Alex's shoulder. "Son, you gonna need more than Joshua's help. You gonna need the Lawd's. Remember dat. I be prayin' for ya."

***

The clickety-clack of horse hooves on the brick driveway caught Alex's attention. He rose from the swing where he had been rereading the telegram from his Uncle Robert. Short but informative, it sent chills of excitement throughout his body:

"Proud of your decision. I welcome my nephew."

The closer the carriage came to the house, the more curious Alex became. It looked as though Sue Ellen and Andrew sat in the back. *But why? They aren't due home until the end of the week.*

Alex ran down the walkway and met the two as the carriage came to a stop.

The second Andrew helped Sue Ellen down from the step, brother and sister wrapped their arms around each other. "Oh, Alex, isn't it awful? Who would have thought war would break out on my honeymoon?" Sue Ellen sniffed in her lady-like

manner. "Andrew thought it best if we returned home early as Saint Augustine is in a turmoil—guns firing, bands playing, folks shouting everywhere." Sue Ellen looked around the grounds. "It's so peaceful here. Where's Father?"

"Atlanta," replied Alex.

"Atlanta? What on earth is he doing in Atlanta?"

"Seems as though he intends to raise hogs for the Confederacy's fightin' men. Someone up there has a breed he wants. You know Father, if there's a penny to be made..."

Andrew joined the conversation and looked at his brother-in-law, "You don't sound too excited about this new venture."

"You're right. That and a few other things Father said before he left. Dinner conversation promises to be more than you expected this evening. Welcome home."

Chapter Nine

"No, no you can't do this, Alex." Sue Ellen's fork slipped from her delicate fingers and clanged against the fine china. "Father will not permit it. He'll accuse you of betraying the Confederacy, as well as your family. Why brother, why?"

Wiping his lips with his napkin, Alex sat up in the oak chair and felt the muscles around his lips grow taut. "Because of my convictions. Our family fought the British to stand together as one nation—not divided into North and South. Our grandfather risked his life to help establish a Republic. I'm willing to risk mine to keep it.

Secession is wrong. I'm willing to bet the elite in every Confederate state that voted to secede will buy their way out of serving on the front lines. Instead, the poorer farmers, middle class merchants, and craftsmen will be sent in to fight. Already Father has figured out a scheme to add to his coffers at the expense of our soldiers. I'm not proud of that." Alex stopped and drained a crystal glass of its water.

Not convinced of her brother's argument, Sue Ellen pushed her plate of unfinished strawberry pie to the side and tugged on Andrew's sleeve. "Andrew, please convince Alex he needs to stay."

Her husband placed a gentle hand over his wife's and replied, "Sweetheart, words cannot always change what's in a man's heart. Alex is convinced, and I might add, with reasonable cause, that he needs to stand for his idea of democracy." Andrew gave Alex a reassuring smile then turned to Sue Ellen. "Remember when we first met, I went through a similar situation with my father."

Sue Ellen's face softened. "Yes, I do recall he wanted you to join him in the mercantile business rather than the clergy. I can still hear him say, "More money in selling to the public than trying to save their souls."

"How did you win him over?" asked Alex.

Andrew sighed. "It wasn't easy, but not unlike your convictions, I knew in my heart and soul that God wanted me to serve Him, not myself. It's a difficult position to be in but your determined actions will speak for themselves."

"Thank you." Alex felt the tension in his face ease. "Your support means much to me."

"Of course," Andrew continued, "when my parents saw that your beautiful sister was willing to give up all of this," he waved his hand about the room, "to settle for a struggling pastor, they accepted my decision." He leaned over and placed a soft kiss on his wife's flushed cheek.

"When will you leave?" Sue Ellen's eyes grew misty.

"In a day or two, before Father returns. I intend to leave him a letter. There's no point in waiting for him. I know better than to light that fuse."

Sue Ellen wiped a meandering tear off her cheek and nodded. "I agree. We've seen how those sparks can multiply, haven't we dear brother?"

***

Flickering rays of light from the dwindling candle fell across a blank sheet of stationary and several balled up sheets of paper lay on the floor beside an oak desk. A throbbing ache in Alex's right temple grew stronger the harder he tried to compose the words into a letter that he knew would drive a permanent wedge between him and his father. Finally, he settled on a composition that was short but direct:

Father,

It is with a heavy heart I write this letter. Recent political events have forced me to stand for my convictions. You accused me of being weak. I intend to prove you wrong. On your arrival, I shall be gone from Oak Haven. My destination is Boston where Uncle Robert has extended his hospitality. In good conscience, I cannot join the Confederacy, but will offer my services to the Union Army.

I pray for your understanding.

Alex

With a steady hand, he inserted the letter into an envelope marked Father, walked to Angus' bedroom and placed it on the nightstand.

Chapter Ten

Joshua flung open the kitchen door and it closed with a slam that caught his mother's attention.

"Lawdy, Son, one of these days the hinges gonna fly right off that door."

"Nah, I be comin' in that door since I's knee-high to a grasshopper and it ain't happen yet." Josh spotted Alex at the table and pointed a finger in his direction. "He run in and out more 'an me."

Alex looked at his friend and laughed as he picked up his breakfast plate and carried it to the sink.

"I confess, I'm as guilty as you, Josh. Used to be you'd paddle our behinds, Mammy. Remember that?" Alex walked over to his friend and gave him a nudge on the shoulder.

Josh nodded, "I 'member it sting, too."

The levity in Alex's voice took on a somber tone and he quizzed Joshua. "Hey, what brings you up to the big house this time of day? If Jenkins catches you up here you're gonna feel the sting of his whip. Do you need somethin'?"

Josh shrugged his shoulders showing little concern. "Aw, I ain't 'fraid of Jenkins today. He nowhere to be seen since your daddy go off. He do it every time the Massa gone. Nobody 'round here gonna tell your daddy. It be our little secret."

Alex snickered, "Won't cross my lips. Fact is I'm glad you're here. I've got something to tell you and I need your help."

Mammy spoke before Alex took another breath. "I swear I not tell 'im. Bin wantin' too but I bites my tongue. You tell 'im."

Joshua looked from his momma back to Alex. "Tell me what?"

Alex took a deep breath. "I'm leaving tonight—going up north to my uncle's. A couple weeks ago I told you Father and I disagreed about secession. Now that war's been declared, I made my mind up. I refuse to fight for the South."

Alex saw the look of despair on his friend's face. Joshua shook his head, his eyes grew misty, and a tremor in his voice caused it to falter, "I's 'fraid it'd come to this. We ever gonna see you again?"

"Hope so. Then again I reckon anything can happen in war. Only the Lord knows for sure."

Alex heard the shuffle of Mammy's feet as she walked to him and placed her hand on his shoulder. She gave him a probing look —one that went beyond a mere glance. "Son, you ready to cross over Jordan?" Without waiting for an answer, she continued, "Mammy done tell you boys all the years you be comin' up that there ain't no second chances once your time on earth is past. You's got to be ready every day."

Alex patted her soft, black, hand. "No need to worry, Mammy. I remember every word—and a few the preacher threw in, too."

***

The setting sun bathed the oaks and pines in a soft, golden glow that lasted for several minutes then turned their statuesque forms into dark shadows. Alex glanced out the bedroom window and saw a rising full moon shining like a silver beacon as if beckoning him to follow the light. It calmed his nerves and he asked himself, *Is this a sign? No clouds tonight. Leaving under cover of darkness shouldn't be so bad after all. Starlight's been to town many times at night.*

Dressed in casual clothes, he thrust last minute items into his knapsack, careful not to carry more than he needed. The last possession he packed was a photo of his parents during their courting years. A rising tide of melancholy threatened to weaken his resolve, so he took one last look around his room and left in haste.

***

CONVICTIONS

Out on the front porch, Sue Ellen and Mammy wept. Andrew paced back and forth trying to counsel them, "Listen, both of you, the last thing Alex needs to see on the faces of the two women he loves is tears. If you can find a dry spot on either of your handkerchiefs , sop 'em up and show him some confidence."

"Yes, 'sa," said Mammy between sobs. "You's right. No need for him to go away with a heavy heart thinkin' we's never gonna see him again."

At the sound of the screen door opening, all eyes turned in Alex's direction. He walked over to Sue Ellen, placed his knapsack on the porch floor, and wrapped his arms around her.

"I'll be on a ship out of Jacksonville in a day or so. There's no way Father can send his hounds to bring me back."

A cry of despair gushed from Mammy's lips and she raised her head up to the ceiling, "Oh, Lawdy, Lawdy, he gonna' drown out on dat ocean. Please save'im."

Andrew said, "Calm down, Mammy. Ships sail up to Boston every day. With the way folks are running around crazy these days, he'll be safer there than on a coach or train."

Brother and sister clung to each other. Neither uttered a word –the time for words had past. Next, Alex felt a tap on his shoulder. He turned toward Andrew who extended his hand and said, "May your heart be at peace. Our prayers go with you." Both men embraced.

Through blurred vision, Alex turned toward Mammy. Her soft whimpering continued as he wrapped his arms around her strong shoulders. This time it was his turn to offer comfort, "No more frettin', Mammy. I'm gonna' be fine. Nobody in this county has more powerful prayers than yours and I know you'll be on your knees every night."

Mammy gave her charge a weak smile and kissed his cheek.

Right on time, the neigh of a horse trotting toward the house distracted those on the porch. Joshua sat with ease on Starlight as he guided the animal to the front lawn. "You take the reins, Alex." Joshua shifted his body to the back of the saddle. "I knows you wants too since no tellin' when you'll see your horse again."

It took little persuasion for Alex to mount Starlight and grab the familiar reins. With one last husky goodbye to his family, he nudged his horse forward and the two young men set out for town. When they reached the main road, Alex turned his body sideways and took a backward, lingering look. The porch lantern light grew dimmer and Oak Haven's size diminished with each step Starlight took. *It's only a house* he reminded himself. *It's the folks inside I'll miss.* With his head held high, Alex spurred Starlight on until the animal settled into a familiar trot.

Chapter Eleven

A rising sun, accompanied by the shrill whistle of a departing train, woke Alex from a shallow sleep. The station's wooden bench he'd chosen to use as a bed was a far cry from the comfort of his feather-filled mattress at Oak Haven. *Oh, well, could've been worse. No tellin' what I'll be sleeping on once I join up with a regiment. Maybe I can catch a few more winks on the train.*

A few winks turned into several hours as the steam-driven engine chugged along the tracks spewing ash and cinders from the inferno blazing inside its boiler. By mid-afternoon, the screech of iron wheels that grated on the metal tracks sent an array of sparks in all directions and the locomotive slowly came to its final destination—Jacksonville.

Alex stepped from the train into an environment filled with an air of excitement. Rebel flags fluttered in the breeze on poles situated on both ends of the station platform while a band beneath one of them played rousing Southern anthems. With the conclusion of each, a crowd of people clapped and cheered. Across the road, a drill sergeant barked orders to a newly formed militia as a spokesman walked up and down the field holding a sign that read, "Beat the Yankees! Join us today!"

Anxious to make his way to the wharf on the St. Johns River, Alex spied an aged black man loading supplies on a wagon and he wandered over to seek directions.

"Hey, can you tell me how to get to the wharf? I need to find passage to Boston?"

The negro, taken back that a white lad had asked for his help, looked into Alex's perspiring face and hesitated before speaking. Alex saw a glimpse of fear in the man's weary eyes and gave him a reassuring smile. "First time I've been here. Don't know my way around."

Finally a rich baritone voice responded. " 'Bout four mile in that direction." He raised an arm and pointed south-east. "I be goin' to the wharf myself. Hitch a ride if ya want."

Alex was quick to accept. "You bet I will. I need to find a captain who'll let me aboard tonight." He threw his satchel up on the wagon then started to pick up a barrel. Before he had a good hold of it, the ole man protested.

"No, no. That my job. You gets dirty. Sit on the seat. I be done soon."

Alex refused. "Two can do the work faster. Besides, this here'll be my thanks."

Within minutes, the creaking old wagon headed toward the smell of the salt water and the squawk of the seagulls. Alex sat quietly as the driver with gnarled, rough-skinned hands talked to his team of horses, guiding them away from the bustle of other wagons and fine carriages that centered around the train depot. Soon the road wound through quiet countryside pasture where herds of cows munched on new shoots of spring grass.

Curiosity urged Alex to start a conversation. "My name's Alex. What's yours?"

For a second there was no response while the man looked at his occupant with a quizzical expression on his glistening black face. Then came, " Sampson."

Alex continued, "Your master live around here?"

This time there was a gentle softening of the muscles around protruding lips. "Ain't gots no massa. I's a freed man. Papers to prove it. Used to have one; a good one, too, but before he die he make me a free man."

Stunned, Alex stumbled over his words. "I'm sorry. I just assumed..."

"Because my skin different than yours?"

Alex nodded. "I never met a freed slave before. My father owns sixty." A hardness entered his next words. "He'd rather die than free a one of them. That's part of the reason I'm leaving.

Can't fight for somethin' I don't believe in. Why do you stay here? You could be up north where there are more like you?"

A genuine smile showed a set of pearl-colored teeth. "I knows all 'bout what goin' on up yonder. This here where I helps my folks. That's all I say 'bout that."

An impromptu gurgle in Alex's stomach reminded him that he hadn't eaten in several hours. He reached into his bag and pulled out a bundle of ham sandwiches Mammy had provided. As he unwrapped the protective cheesecloth, Alex offered one to Sampson. Reluctant to take the young man's food, he shook his head.

Alex persisted, "C'mon now, you must be hungry. Besides, my Mammy makes the best vittles in our county. She'd take a switch to me if she thought I hoarded them to myself and didn't share."

A ripple of laughter erupted from Sampson as he reached for a sandwich. "Sound like ma Mammy. You ain't got no mama?"

"Died during my birth. Mammy raised me. Her son, Joshua's my best friend." Alex dropped his chin and his voice grew somber. "Hated saying good-bye at the station in Tallahassee but God- willing we'll meet again after this here fightin's done."

The two rode in silence chewing on the ham that satisfied their hunger. After a few minutes, Alex noticed the elevation of the land changed and became flatter. The tall masts of ships were visible and before long glistening water danced before his eyes.

Sampson saw the anticipation on Alex's face and he said, "I can get you aboard a ship. Fact is we be haulin' supplies for the 'Emerald Lady'. Captain Darcy and me work together. You let me do the talkin', hear?"

The wagon came to a stop on the wharf next to a sailing ship that was being loaded with bales of cotton. Prancing up and down the deck giving directions was a short, wiry fellow smoking a pipe. Curly red hair sprung like corkscrews from beneath his captain's cap.

"Aye, Sampson", he shouted, "be right with you." Spry legs hopped over mooring ropes and landed him on the wharf. "And who do we have here?" Sparkling green eyes surveyed Alex from top to bottom.

"New cabin boy. Alex his name," said Sampson. "He bound for Boston."

Alex looked at Sampson in surprise. *Cabin boy? But I've never been on a ship.*

Captain Darcy gave him a hearty handshake. "Welcome aboard, lad." Alex soon detected the Irish brogue. "The last one left me to join the Rebs. It's a sorry mess we're in. Go ahead and store your gear below. Ask that fella in the blue shirt to show you 'round."

Alex turned to Sampson. "Mighty grateful for your help."

"Ain't nothin'." Two black hands grasped hold of Alex's arm and held it fast. "You take care now. Ole Sampson see dark days ahead but I believes you done right."

***

By nightfall, sailors on the *Emerald Lady* cast off mooring ropes and set her free to follow the St. John's River to the Atlantic Ocean. Too excited to sleep, Alex tossed and turned in his hammock. Little fresh air flowed through the crammed lower deck that housed the crew and beads of perspiration formed on Alex's forehead. A nauseous feeling encouraged him to get to the top deck immediately. After emptying the contents of his stomach overboard, he slowly savored the long breaths of sea air as he looked across the moonlit water. His eyes strained to focus on a moving object that maneuvered its way toward the ship. The sound of paddles slapping water caused his ears to perk up and listen for any other identifying sounds—a murmur of voices, one an Irish lilt to it, another the diction of a black man.

What's happening? Alex inched closer hidden by the shadows. In seconds, a lone man on deck threw a rope ladder over the side and soon, one by one, three adults and a child each emerged from below to step foot on ship.

Stow-aways? Alex's pulse beat faster. *But who are they? And why?*

CONVICTIONS

The mystery solved itself as he heard the Captain say to the newcomers, "Welcome aboard—your first step to freedom. Now quickly down into the hold."

Once again Alex listened to the retreating sound of a rowboat and the scene played out before him proclaimed the truth. *I'm part of an illegal, slave runner vessel. If we're caught, it's cause for treason. This isn't the voyage I planned, but,* Alex looked ahead at the approaching Atlantic, *it's too late now.*

Chapter Twelve

Alex rolled out of his hammock at dawn and tried to stand. Each time he stood, the swaying of the ship caught him off balance and threw him onto the floor. After several more attempts, he learned to get in sync with the rhythm of the waves and staggered into the galley.

The cook took one look at Alex's pale, haggard face and his rotund belly shook with laughter. "Aye, never been to sea, lad, have you?"

"No, sir. First time."

"Then we need to get you in shape." He reached into a cupboard, grabbed a ginger root and handed it to Alex. "Chew on this herb. Calms the stomach and lets you eat. You need to gnaw on a biscuit, too. Always keep one in your pocket and nibble on it throughout the day until you can keep it all down."

Appreciative of the cook's advice, Alex thanked him and asked, "When does the Captain eat breakfast? I'm to deliver it to his cabin, right?"

"His pot of tea is ready. He'll eat two biscuits with honey. Think you can handle this basket? I can call one of the mates to help until you get your sea legs."

Alex reached for the basket. "No, it's my responsibility." A feeble smile crossed his lips. " You'll see; I'll be dancing a jig before we reach Boston."

"Aye, now that's a good lad."

Alex struggled to keep his balance against the wind and the never-ending waves as he stumbled across several yards to the Captain's quarters. He heard the slosh of the tea in the pewter pot as it threatened to spill its contents. With a sigh of relief he reached the door and knocked. Within seconds, Captain Darcy unlatched the lock and Alex stepped inside.

"Good morning, sir. My apology if I'm late. I need some adjusting to sea life."

Captain Darcy chuckled. "It's mostly mind over matter, son. Here sit and have a cup of tea. Tell me about yourself. Something tells me you're on the run."

Alex felt a sudden flush of fear surge through his body. *Why is he interested in my affairs? Will he try to send me back?* A moment of silence followed before he spoke.

"It's a long story, Captain."

"And it's a long voyage. I have time."

Alex looked into the Captain's relaxed, weathered face and he felt a sense of calmness he hadn't felt for months. For over a half-hour, his words told the story of his life and how he vowed to fight to keep the Union as the Founders intended.

Captain Darcy reached over and patted Alex on the arm before stating, "We're of like mind, lad. My family crossed the Atlantic during the potato famine in Ireland and settled in Massachusetts. I come from a line of ship builders. The *Emerald Lady* is one my grandfather helped build." The Captain took a deep breath and squared his shoulders. " I'm proud to be its Captain. Like you, Alex, I believe in one Union. I'm too old to fight but there are other ways to show my allegiance."

"Is helping slaves escape what you mean?"

Alex saw the expression on Captain Darcy's face turn from surprise to cold seriousness. "Why do you ask?"

Oh, no, Alex felt his pulse quicken. *I should have kept silent. It's not my business. Now I'll have to confess what I saw.*

"Late last night my stomach turned sour. I scurried to the upper deck and retched over the side of the ship. While gasping for fresh air, I saw the rowboat approach and three adults and a child climb aboard. You instructed them to get down into the hold. I've heard of run-away slaves stowing on ships going north," Alex paused before he continued, "but I didn't know I'd be on one."

"Can I count on you to keep what you saw a secret?" The Captain's eyes searched Alex's face for assurance. "I'm not the only one who'll suffer if the truth be known. These things take planning and others are involved—like Sampson. He rowed the boat."

"Ah, so what you're doing is akin to the rumors we hear about an underground railroad helping Negroes flee from the south. You have my word, Captain." Alex extended his hand to shake on the promise. "But I have questions."

"Feel free to ask."

"Do the sailors on board know there are fugitives in the hold?"

"Yes. I pick my crew carefully. They are part of the team."

"Have you ever been searched?"

"Once. But we outwitted the authorities. Black men make good sailors, too."

"Why have you not converted to steam like so many others? It seems to me your chances of out-running other ships would be to your advantage. You could get to Boston in less time."

A twinkle crept back into the Captain's eyes. "That's the whole idea, lad. Since the Emerald Lady is smaller and slower, dependent on favorable winds to sail, they don't suspect we'd take a chance of carrying run-aways. It's the pirates that give me troubles. They steal the cotton and sell it on the black market. Unscrupulous men they are." He turned toward a shelf laden with weapons. "I trust your military school taught you how to shoot a gun?"

"Yes, sir. Self- defense was high priority."

"Good. Should the need arise, you take any of these guns and arm yourself."

"I will, sir."

"Now," Captain Darcy drained the remainder of the tea in his cup, stood up and gave Alex instructions. "You need to learn how to assist the men with their chores while you're mastering your sea-legs. Watch how they maintain the sails, tie the ropes, scrub the decks. Anything that will keep your mind busy. I eat with the crew at noon so get out there and show my men what you're made of."

"I'll give it my best, Captain." Alex cleared the table. With basket in hand, he made his way back to the galley. With every staggering step he repeated, "I can do this. I can do this." Another thought brought urgency to his task. *Pirates? Guns? Swords? Oh yes, I have no choice.*

Chapter Thirteen

After seven days at sea, hunger pains replaced the uneasy nauseous feeling in the pit of Alex's stomach. His legs no longer buckled under him when he stood or walked and he looked forward to mingling with the other crew members. His change of mood did not go unnoticed among the men as he carried breakfast to the Captain's quarters.

"Aye, lad, I can see you're looking chipper this morn'," said one of the sailors. " Got some color back in yer face. I was begin' to think we'd be having a sea burial if you didn't soon show signs of life." The man's hearty laughter and humor encouraged others to join in.

Alex shrugged it off. " I admit I was useless last week but I'm ready to tackle whatever needs done today." He surveyed the upper deck and scouted for a job to do. The first thing he noticed was the first mate on the bridge looking off into the distance with his telescope. Seconds later, he handed the instrument to the helmsman who put it to his right eye, held it for a few seconds, then nodded as he handed it back to the first mate. *What are they seeing?* wondered Alex. *There's nothing but water everywhere I look.*

Just as Alex put his knuckles to the Captain's door to knock, it opened and Captain Darcy ushered him in. "Ah, I thought you'd gotten lost this morning, son."

Alex felt guilt sting his conscience and explained, "Forgive me, Captain, but the actions of the first mate caught my eye and I stopped to watch."

"And what was he doing?"

"Looking out to sea with his telescope."

"That's his job—to look for and identify other ships."

Alex arranged the tea and biscuits on the table before responding. "I think he and the helmsman spotted one."

Captain Darcy raised his eyebrows and curiosity lit up his face. "Well, now," he poured a cup of tea and said, "we'll watch for its flag's identity. We're heading into dangerous territory. Pirates. With this fair weather and the help of the Gulf Stream we've covered a good distance, so according to my calculations we're off the South Carolina coast where those dirty rascals linger waiting for merchant ships to pass. I heard rumors, too, while we were in port that the Union intends to put up a blockade. That will keep the south from sending cotton to Europe as well as stop supply ships from aiding the Confederates." A sly smile crinkled the edges of the captain's mouth. "Life on the sea is going to get interesting."

***

All afternoon, Alex detected murmurings among the sailors that the Emerald Lady was being tracked by another ship. He scanned the horizon and his eyes focused on a speck that in his mind had the shape of a sea-going vessel. But it was much too far away to identify with his naked eye. What he did recognize was a change in the clouds. No longer were wispy, white balls of fluff dancing against an azure background but masses of graying vapor congregated to form thunder heads. A drop in the temperature and blasts of agitated wind swirling above the water increased the height of waves that lashed against the *Emerald Lady*.

"Quickly, lad," ordered one of the mates, "gather anything lying loose. Stow it below deck before a wave washes over and we lose our tools."

It took several trips to grab and deposit mops, buckets, sail-mending gear, and coils of rope. Thunder warned of an approaching storm and each time the rumble grew louder and louder.

Sporadic drops of rain splattered on the upper deck while lightening zigzagged across the darkening sky.

Mesmerized by the sight before him, Alex stood for twenty minutes watching the bare-footed sailors climb the rigging, battening down flapping sails while a man in the crow's nest kept watch of the approaching ship. Flashes of lightening came closer forcing him to scurry down the ropes to safety.

Alex soon became drenched with a mixture of sea water and rain. Still he did not move. Suddenly he felt the *Emerald Lady* roll, his feet came out from under him and he fell on his stomach. A surge of water swept his body across the deck until he stopped at the feet of the captain.

With an awkward movement, he tried to get up as another wave caused the ship to take an unexpected dive. This time, a strong arm supported his unsteady body and he heard, "Into my cabin before you get swept overboard!"

"Yes, sir." With no delay, Alex sought shelter.

By the time Captain Darcy entered his quarters, a puddle of water surrounded Alex. The Commander took one look at his cabin boy, opened a wooden chest and threw a shirt and a pair of bloomer-style pants in his direction. "Here, put these on. Next time there's a storm I want you below. Stay out of the way; you could have been injured."

Alex hung his head in contrition, "I should have known better. It won't happen again, sir."

While Alex changed his clothes, Captain Darcy paced the deck. His bushy eyebrows knit together in a gesture of concern as he pawed at his beard. Alex sensed more than a storm was on the commander's mind. *Dare I ask?* After another five minutes of this behavior, he blurted, "Captain, I can see you're upset and I believe it's more than my foolish behavior. Is there anything I can do for you?"

The captain circled the room once more then seated himself at the table. "Sit, Alex. My men have spotted a ship advancing in our direction. It appears as though she's flying respectable colors—possibly British."

"That's good, is it not? We no longer fear their fleet, do we?"

"It may be a trick. Pirates fly other countries' flags in order to deceive merchant ships, then when they think they are close enough to attack, they run up the Jolly Roger. It's a ploy to intimidate a ship's crew into handing over cargo, men, sometimes the ship itself."

Alex listened to tactics he'd only read about in books. "What do we do, Captain?" His breathing accelerated as his mind raced with images of battle on the sea.

"Can we outrun them?"

"Not likely. They've been sailing at several knots more than we are capable of moving. Our cotton slows us down but I suspect their hold is empty—ready to be filled with our cargo." Captain Darcy shook his head and placed his right hand over his heart. " Aye, as sure as my soul is Irish, my gut tells me there'll be a fracas on our hands before long." He turned to the wall of weapons and stretched his right arm toward the armaments. "Pick one you can handle then take it below. Should the need arise to fire it, take careful aim. You may get only one chance."

Alex scanned the assortment of guns then spoke. "I have my own revolver, sir. Brought it from home. Fact is, I almost used it on a foreman who mistreated one of the slaves not long ago. I appreciate the forewarning though. Should I speak to the negroes? I suspect they've got some good fight in them if needed?"

"Tell 'em to be on guard. No need to get involved if they don't have to."

With a nod, Alex picked up his wet clothing and started toward the door. The last words he heard Captain Darcy mutter were, "T'will be a cold day in Hades when I give up Grandfather's ship."

Chapter Fourteen

For the next hour, Alex lay in the swaying hammock with his Colt revolver tucked into the waistband of the baggy britches. Random thoughts darted from one scenario to another. *What if the Captain's concern is real? Can I defend myself? Will the skills I learned at military school hold true?* No one is pretending here. Alex forced himself to take deep breaths to calm his nerves. As he did so, he closed his eyes and Mammy's shining, black face erased the earlier chaotic visions. He heard her words in his mind command him. "Pray to the Almighty. He will provide a shield of protection." As quickly as she came, she was gone, but Alex knew he'd been touched by her spirit and responded with a prayer for safety. From deep below, as if on cue, he heard faint, soothing, voices singing a Negro spiritual. But not for long. The boom of a canon shattered the melodic sound and the ship's timbers shivered.

Alex sat up and raised his head to the small deck prism that kept his quarters from complete darkness. *Are we being attacked?* Rivulets of water ran down the glass obscuring a clear view but he recognized human forms running through a mixture of smoke and mist. A clamor of voices and clashing of swords broke the rhythmical pattern of the rain.

Above the din, a deep- throated, unfamiliar authoritative figure caught Alex's attention and he crawled up to the hatch, opened it just enough to see who was issuing orders. Standing beside a grappling rope on the starboard side stood a long-haired, tall, bearded scoundrel with his left arm around Captain Darcy's neck. In his right hand, he brandished a gleaming knife pressed against the Captain's throat.

A sickening chill ran through Alex's body when he heard the words, "Mates, if you don't want to see your captain slain before your eyes, listen to my orders. We know the *Emerald Lady* has cotton in the hold. I want it. Rumor has it something more valuable than cotton is hidden there, too." His coarse laughter rang out into the wind. "Slaves. Big money. Now step aside, put down your weapons and start emptying the hold." To emphasize his threat, the pirate took the knife and drew it beneath Captain Darcy's chin.

"No, take me," yelled the first mate as he started toward the Captain. In seconds, a dagger lodged between his shoulder blades and he crumbled to the deck.

Alex heard Captain Darcy's wail followed by a string of curses. *Who'll be next?* he wondered. Without hesitation, he withdrew his revolver from beneath his smock and cocked it. To his surprise, the three black men emerged from the hold each with an axe in their hand. They motioned for him to keep quiet. The leader whispered, "We get the pirate's attention. You shoot the leader in the head. Don't miss. He kill the Captain."

Alex nodded. Adrenaline surged through his body but he sighted his Colt on the red bandana worn by the enemy. The black man pushed the hatch open and all three jumped onto the deck yelling, screaming, and waving their axes in the air like savages. The moment the pirate's leader looked in their direction, Alex squeezed the trigger. For a few seconds he couldn't breathe. *Did I hit him?* Immediate relief came when he saw blood gush from the man's temple, his body slump forward, and the knife drop from his hand to the deck.

Fear gripped the other pirates and they released knives, revolvers, and swords. Captain Darcy, back in command, shouted, "All prisoners bound and taken to the brig."

Tears rolled down the Captain's face as he dislodged the dagger from his first mate's back. Blood ran from the wound in an unending stream. His breathing came in erratic spasms and finally stopped. Alex walked to the side of the ship and threw up.

CONVICTIONS

***

As the clouds parted and the evening sun sank below the horizon, Captain Darcy ordered the pirate vessel torched. Light from the burning ship drew Alex to the upper deck. The *Emerald Lady* set sail and left the carnage to sink into the sea. Alex was deep in thought, the day's nightmare still fresh on his mind and didn't hear footsteps come up behind him. He flinched when a hand wrapped around his shoulders. A familiar voice said, "Thank you for saving my life, Alex. Jonah, one of the slaves told me of your bravery. I'm forever in your debt."

"No sir. It was my duty." Alex could no longer contain the emotion stirring inside him. "I've never killed a man, but I'm not sorry I did. And today was the first time I've seen a man die." His voice trembled and he wiped away the flowing tears.

"And it won't be the last, lad. You're going to war and war means death. It's going to be all around you. It's a hard lesson, but I believe you came a long way today. One thing I know for sure…"

Alex cut in, "What's that, sir?"

"You're a great shot. The Rebs don't know what they're missing."

Chapter Fifteen

With the threat of pirates behind the *Emerald Lady*, Captain Darcy announced to Alex after breakfast, "Tell Jonah and his people to feel free to leave the hold and come up on deck. T'is mighty cramped down there. Some fresh salty air and sunshine will do 'em all some good."

"But, Captain, is it safe for them to be seen should we be spotted again?"

"Ah, no worry, lad. We're approaching northern waters and the pirates lose their nerve when they recognize a Union Navy ship patrolling the coast. They know the cannons on board can blast their ships to splinters with the light of a fuse." Captain Darcy reclined in his chair, lit his pipe and sighed, " No, I feel we're safe now. Barring natural disasters, in a week or so we should be in Boston harbor and I'll be enjoying a pint or two with my friends in O'Shaunessy's pub. You're welcome to join us."

***

The Negroes wasted no time in finding their way to the upper deck after Alex delivered the Captain's message—especially the young boy. He bounded up the steps and ran from one side of the ship to the other. Because of his close connections with the slaves on Oak Haven, Alex felt comfortable talking and mingling with them.

"Jonah," he said, "I'm amazed at the bravery you showed against the pirates. Without it, there's a good chance we all could be under a different commander today."

"We's use to fightin' for our survival. We knowed we be split up and sold somewhere in the islands if dat wicked man have his way. I loves my family. Don't want that to happen so we got a plan."

"And what's that? Is it secret?"

"I tells you 'cause you proved you'se the right kind of man. We go to a place called Nova Scotia. In Canada. There be free black folk live there."

Jonah held Alex's attention. "Canada? That's a long way from Boston. How are you going to do that?"

Jonah lowered his voice. "Captain tell me we sail into Boston at night. There be men who spend their time lookin' for run-away slaves so it not safe to hang around on shore. Just like Sampson help us find the *Emerald Lady*, someone take us to another ship that sail to Canada."

"But you could stay in the Union and be free, too."

Jonah removed his straw hat and ran his fingers through coarse black hair before answering. To Alex, the look in his friend's eyes suggested he might be mulling over options then he said, " No, I always be lookin' back 'fraid those vigilantes put a rope 'round my neck. 'Sides, lots of folks say Massa Lincoln ain't fightin' this war for us black folks, anyways. They say he wants to teach the South a lesson—show the Confederates who be the stronger."

"There may be some truth in that," agreed Alex as he slid a mop up and down the deck planking, "but as one Union we all stay strong—just like it says in the Bible. Each of our body parts work together to make one whole. Can you imagine if one day your legs said, 'I'm tired of listening to the brain tell me how to move. I'll just not budge. Then the eyes refuse to open and your arms decide to hang uselessly from your shoulders.' You'd be in bad shape, wouldn't you?"

Jonah chuckled at the analogy. "I needs all my parts workin' but I see's what you mean, Alex. Maybe someday when all this get straighten out we come back." A big sigh crossed his lips, "Maybe not."

Chapter Sixteen

With each passing day, Alex felt subtle changes in the environment that indicated the *Emerald Lady* was closer to her destination. Even though it was almost the beginning of May, the air was cooler and the sun's rays weaker than in the south. The ship sailed nearer to the coastline and every now and then he saw a lighthouse sitting on a rocky cliff warning vessels that danger lurked below the ocean's surface. The sailors whistled cheery tunes in anticipation of celebrating another successful voyage with friends and loved ones.

As the afternoon slipped into early evening, Captain Darcy ordered all hands on deck to stow unneeded equipment while the *Emerald Lady* prepared to sail into Boston Harbor. He walked over to where Alex coiled a rope. "We won't be docking until dawn. Our anchor will keep us at the mouth of the harbor where we'll spend the night. Except for Jonah and his folks. Soon as it's past midnight they'll be picked up and taken to another ship that's waiting for them."

Alex nodded. "He told me they can't go ashore. I suspect there's big money in returning run-aways, but can you trust whoever meets us?"

"Truth be known, lad, I don't trust nobody these days. That's why there'll be a skiff lowered over port side in case an escape is necessary."

Alex finished his task, then stood before the Captain, "Then what do they do?"

Captain Darcy gave Alex a good-natured slap on his shoulder. "We hope they know how to row."

***

Alex tossed and turned in his hammock unable to sleep. It wasn't the excessive snoring or guttural sounds from the crew around him that kept him awake, he was used to that annoyance, but excitement ignited the nerves in his body. He wanted to see the slaves safely depart for their journey to Canada.

At the appointed time, he heard Jonah and his family come up from the hold and make their way to the upper deck. He followed, careful not to disturb the other sleeping men.

Along with Captain Darcy, two other sailors stood ready to assist the slaves down the rope ladder. Alex walked over to the Captain and said, "Couldn't sleep, sir. And I wanted to see them off."

"Here." He handed Alex the telescope, "tell me if you can spot movement in the water coming toward us. It looks like a small vessel but by now I should see the code."

"Code, sir?"

"Yes, we use lantern signals to identify the freedom boat. Then I respond to tell them we're ready."

Alex put the instrument up to his right eye and carefully scanned the moonlit surface until he focused on an object that bobbed on the choppy water. Long wooden arms protruded from each side and they moved in tandem as two men put all their strength into rowing the boat. With each dip of the oars, they came closer to the *Emerald Lady*.

"It's a row boat, sir. Don't see any sign of light."

Captain Darcy took the telescope. "Somethin's not right. They don't want to be seen by other vessels. My gut tells me they plan to harm—not help. Vigilantes lookin' fer run-aways."

The slaves gasped in alarm.

"Jonah, quick, you go first. Move to the port side, climb down the ladder and get into the skiff. Two men row. The rest of you lay on the bottom." Captain Darcy's words softened, "This wasn't supposed to happen. You're on your own now. Be careful to follow the coast so you don't row out to sea. The North star will guide you." He gave Jonah a reassuring pat on the back then turned to Alex. "You need to go, too. These men will be armed and angry when they see no slaves. No tellin' what they'll do."

"But, but—"

"No arguing, lad, it's for your own good. No time to waste." As Alex stepped over the ship onto the first rung of the ladder, Captain Darcy grabbed his arm and said, "I'm proud of you, lad. You made a good sailor and I know you'll be a fine soldier. The saints be with you."

Chapter Seventeen

Once settled in the rowboat, the shaken group uttered not a word but listened as waves lapped against the wooden frame. *No, no this can't be,* thought Alex, *I've come too far to drown so close to my destination. Nor will I be captured by a band of thugs.* He reached for his revolver and felt the assurance of the cold steel against his thigh.

From the back of the boat, came a woman's soft weeping. A swell of empathy pulled at Alex's heart. *What must she be thinking? Her dreams of escape shattered? Is she terrified she'll lose her life, her husband, her son?*

Alex saw the loving arm of her husband draw her close and he heard words of comfort. "It be fine, Lily Mae. There be another time. Another ship to Canada. You got's to be strong. The Lord, He up there watching us—leading us away from danger. Talk to him baby. I believes He love to hear your prayers."

The other two black men took hold of the oars and began to row several yards into the darkness. Ten minutes later, the skiff's occupants heard gunshots pierce the night's stillness. The oarsmen dug their paddles deeper into the water and the skiff left a small wake behind. *What happened on the Emerald Lady? Who won't see tomorrow? Will I ever know?*

Following Captain Darcy's instructions, he looked to the North Star to get their bearings then instructed the men to turn west. His watering eyes strained to see any sign of life. *Was that a flicker of light high in the air?* Alex kept his eyes on the object while the men rowed faster and faster toward the shore. *A lighthouse maybe? A light from a church steeple?*

Although the hour was late, more and more illumination shone from sporadic locations. Jonah noticed a change too and his spirits rose. "We's must be close to Boston." He leaned closer to the oarsmen. "Be careful. Never know what hidin' under da water. Don't need no rock wreckin' a hole in the boat."

"I'm watchin' for danger, Jonah," answered Alex from the bow. "Not easy to see in the dark. Take it slow now."

Within the hour, night surrendered to a hallowed-like glow that slowly rose from the horizon to lighten the waiting sky. The Boston shoreline was a welcomed relief to the weary passengers aboard the sturdy skiff. They saw curling smoke from chimney tops dissipate into the crisp morning air as inhabitants inside two-story brick homes began breakfast preparation. The rhythmic sound of horses' hooves stepping on cobblestone streets echoed across the calm water. Like a bear emerging from a long winter's sleep, Boston came alive—stretched, yawned and embraced a new day after a night of rest.

Alex and Jonah scanned the shoreline for some inconspicuous spot where they might find cover from curious onlookers. A short distance from the main wharf a small cove surrounded by hemlock and spruce evergreens looked as though it offered a safe haven.

Alex felt relief as he stepped onto solid ground after so many days on the water. His exhausted body wanted nothing more than to lie on the sweet-smelling earth and drift into a deep sleep. But reality fought for reason. They needed nourishment and shelter, and he knew Alex McPhail was now the slaves' only hope of surviving this ordeal. *How did I become their protector?* Instantly, his spirits rose. *Uncle Robert, of course. He'll be willing to help them.*

"Jonah," Alex stepped up to the disillusioned black man and squeezed his arm. "I'm going for help and I need you to come with me."

"Where you take me? T'aint gonna leave my family."

"To my uncle's. He's a lawyer in town and he'll know what to do. If nothing else, I know he'll feed us." Alex continued his pleading, "Nobody's going to take you in broad daylight. We're not in the South anymore."

It appeared to Alex that Jonah's tense muscles relaxed and a spark of life lit up his chestnut-brown eyes. "I's ready."

"You're a good man, my friend. First, we need to hide the skiff. We'll pull it up under these spruce branches where it'll blend in." With that task completed, Alex turned to the rest of the group. "Spread out and keep close to the trees. We'll be back as soon as possible."

Lilly Mae ran to Jonah and threw her arms around him. "I's scared, husband. We's a long way from home. What we do without cha?"

"My brothers here ain't gonna let no harm come to you and our chile. I needs you be strong." He gave his wife a warm hug then turned to Alex. "C'mon, let's find your kin."

***

On a dusty road that led into the city, strangers riding on horses or sitting in fancy carriages stared at the young white man with the disheveled hair and clothes walking with a barefoot black man in tattered overalls. Determination powered each step while the rumbling of hunger pangs gnawed at their stomachs and thirst dried the membranes of their throats. The closer they came to the city, the larger Jonah's eyes grew until he couldn't contain his amazement. "Lawdy, lawdy, I never seen such sights! People everywhere. Why they in such a hurry? Where they go?"

At that moment a shrill whistle blared into the morning air as throngs of men, women, and children rushed up the steps to the mills where the sound of industry purred and banged. Alex explained, "Even though these folk don't work the cotton fields, like you did, Jonah, they spend hours inside those buildings hunched over machines that turn the cotton into yards and yards of material."

"Don't sound like much difference to me. They gots a boss watchin' 'em?"

"Oh yes. He sees that the workers put in a good day's work."

"Well, what make it better?"

"Freedom. No chains, no whips. They're even paid to work. They have a chance to make a better life for their families. That's what you want, don't you?"

"Sho do. I knows I's one of the lucky ones to reach the north. Don't know what gonna happen but I wants to help my people like Sampson help me." Jonah adjusted his pine straw hat against a gust of wind that threatened to blow it off.

"Stick around in these parts and you'll probably get a chance to do that."

"How?"

"Ever hear of the Underground Railroad?"

"What you mean underground? Trains run on tracks 'bove the ground."

Alex chuckled. "You're right, Jonah, but this really doesn't mean what it sounds like."

"Now you teasin' me. I be confused."

"It's true. A secret movement has sprung up where run-aways find safe houses to help them all the way from the deep south to the northern states. Kinda like what Captain Darcy did for you and your folks."

"Ahh," said Jonah as he nodded. "That take courage to help slaves. How you know about dis?"

"I overheard my father's friends tell him about it. Warned him to take count of his slaves every night least someone come up missing. And listen to this."

Jonah turned to face his companion, not wanting to miss a word. "I listen."

"This whole idea started with a woman. Her name is Harriet Tubman." Alex smiled at Jonah's reaction.

"No. Ain't no woman could do such thing. Now I knows you teasin'."

"Better not let Lilly Mae hear that talk come across your lips, my man, or you'll be wishing you'd shut your mouth."

Jonah chuckled before he pleaded Alex's confidence. "That be a little secret 'tween you and me, okay, Alex?"

A smile parted Alex's lips. "She won't hear it from me, friend, you got my word." He wiped the back of his hand across his forehead, already damp with sweat.

"Hey, man, the sun's startin' to climb and we need to find my uncle before we dry up and turn to dust. No time to waste. Keep one foot in front of the other."

Chapter Eighteen

Leaving the industrial mills that stood alongside the Charles River, Alex and Jonah entered the business district of Boston with its multitude of row-styled brick buildings. Wooden shingles of all shapes and sizes hung from above each door advertising the establishment's merchandise. Dry goods, eateries, bakeries, meat markets, pubs, millinery shops, ladies clothing, ship supply stores, and apothecaries lined the streets. But nowhere did Alex read a sign that spelled Robert McPhail Attorney at Law.

Tired of walking through a maze, he stepped inside a barber shop and inquired of a man sharpening razors, " Excuse me, sir, I'm looking for the office of attorney Robert McPhail. Can you direct me?"

The barber looked at the two misfits standing before him. His eyes surveyed their appearance, then answered with a question of his own, "And who may I ask are you?"

"Alex McPhail, his nephew, and this is Jonah. We arrived from Florida by ship last night. My uncle is expecting me."

The muscles around the barber's mouth relaxed into a warm smile. "Ah, so you're the lad he told me about. He was in last week. I trim his moustache and goatee." A baritone chuckle gurgled up from his throat. " Can't do much for his hair; he's bald on top. All's left is a little fringe around his ears."

Not wishing to linger discussing his uncle's appearance, Alex asked again, "The name of the street, sir, where do I find him?"

"C'mon, step outside and I'll set you in the right direction. It's not far."

By now it was close to high noon and the glare of the sun

forced the men to shade their eyes as the barber pointed off in the distance. "See the spire above the trees; that's Federal Street Church. Your uncle's office is directly across from it. You best hurry. He likes to walk home for lunch."

Alex offered his hand to the barber, "We appreciate your kindness, sir. I'll be sure to tell Uncle Robert."

The man shook his head in protest, "Nay, 'tis not necessary. Just tell him I'll be at the meeting tonight." A gush of exuberance in his voice announced, "Say, you and Jonah might find it of interest, too."

Puzzled, Alex asked, "What kind of meeting?"

"Abolitionism—your uncle is one of us, lad."

***

Alex and Jonah walked in silence toward the church when suddenly Jonah said, "What that man mean, abolitionism? Never heard that word. It good or bad?"

"I reckon it depends if you're for or against it. Some folks in the south, like my father and his friends, don't care for it 'cause it means to abolish, get rid of slavery."

"Why that be a good thing—if'un you be a slave."

"Well, there's a group up here in the north who agree with you and they're trying to convince President Lincoln to pass a law to free y'all. They're called Abolitionists." Alex's voice tingled with excitement. "Never thought Uncle Robert was one of them but I guess we'll soon find out. Let's hurry, Jonah. If we catch him soon enough we might get a lunch invitation. I know my stomach sure could use one."

Chapter Nineteen

The sound of church bells reverberated through the air and echoed in Alex and Jonah's ears. One chime after the other rang until there was silence.

"What dat noise, Alex? I's never hear dat sound before. I knowed the Bible tell us de Lawd come back with the sound of a trumpet," Jonah looked heavenward, "but I don' sees Him and that weren't no trumpet."

Alex laughed, "The big churches up here build steeples and hang a huge bell with a rope tied to it. Every hour a man climbs up and pulls on the rope so it makes a clanging noise to let folks know the time of day. I counted twelve rings so it's noon. Let's hope Uncle Robert hasn't left his office yet."

No sooner had Alex uttered his concern when the church came in sight and across the street a man in a stove-pipe hat, waistcoat and sporting a waxed mustache stepped out onto the steps of a building. He proceeded to lock the door. Hanging above him a swinging sign read, 'Robert McPhail, Attorney at Law'.

Alex broke into a run, "Uncle Robert, wait!"

Startled by the sudden vocal eruption, Robert turned and asked, "Do I know you?"

"It's Alex, sir. Your nephew."

Robert's eyes scanned the bedraggled-looking young man for a few seconds before speaking.

Alex held his breath. *What if he doesn't believe me? I'm a stranger to him. He's never seen me until now. Please don't turn me away.*

Robert saw the pleading in his nephew's eyes and reassured

him. "By jove, you do favor your father. The cheekbones and ruddy complexion. But I didn't expect a lad in tattered shirt and baggy britches. Where are your belongings? And who is your companion?"

Alex sighed and he grabbed Jonah's arm and pulled him forward. "This is Jonah, sir. We have a long story to tell and are in desperate need of help."

Robert slung an arm around Alex's shoulder and welcomed him heartily. "We've been expecting you for a week or more. Your cousins, Jenny and Coreen are beside themselves waiting for you. Tell me what's happened since you left the plantation?"

Alex summarized events, leaving out the finer details until later. Right now, he needed help rescuing the four Negroes left at the cove.

"I must say your voyage piqued my interest. Excitement from beginning to end." Robert gave Jonah a confident smile. "Come, we'll tarry no longer. The livery stable is down by the wharf. I'll rent a wagon and we'll fetch your folks. There's a safe house near the shore where you can rest until you decide where you want to go."

Robert saw glistening tears of gratitude trickle down Jonah's face. The black man tried to speak but his words kept getting caught in his throat so he grasped the lawyer's hand and squeezed it with all his might.

***

While Jonah took hold of the horse's reins, Alex directed him to follow the dusty road they'd traveled earlier . Robert asked question after question. How did the slaves board the ship undetected? Was the weather favorable or did they face any storms? Did you get seasick? Were the rations edible? Who was your Captain and what was the name of his ship?

"Captain Darcy. *The Emerald Lady.*"

"No," replied Robert, his voice gaining volume as he caught hold of Alex's arm. "Mercy, mercy."

"What's wrong Uncle?"

"Of course," Robert said. "You wouldn't know since you jumped ship in the middle of the night."

A dreaded feeling in the pit of Alex's stomach sensed that something was wrong. "Know what, Uncle?"

Robert took a deep breath and said, "Captain Darcy's dead. The rogues who sought you and your kin shot him when he refused to disclose your where-abouts. News came to me early this morning from a sailor who was on board. I'm part of the freedom network. I knew the captain well. We've shared many a pint at O'Shaunessey's."

Alex and Jonah looked at each other in disbelief. Jonah broke down first. "Can't be; I owes my life to da Captain." Again, his eyes filled with pools of water and meandering tears covered his cheeks. "Oh, Lawdy, Lawdy."

"That explains it," recalled Alex. "I heard shots in the distance as we rowed toward shore." A tremble in his voice exposed his emotions. "Captain Darcy's courage leaves much to live up to." Alex took a deep breath and continued, "I owe him my freedom, too."

For the next few minutes the three men rode in silence. Each mourned the death of a friend until Alex recognized the area where the slaves hid. The road came to a dead end in an open field where tilled soil lay ready for planting. Beyond, evergreen trees with thick, barrel-like trunks and heavily needled branches stretched skyward.

Alex took command, "Wait here, Uncle. Jonah and I will run get his kin. If they stayed where we left them, we shouldn't be long. I trust Aunt Abigail won't worry that you're late for your mid-day meal."

"It won't be the first time, son. She understands my commitment to help these poor, black souls. Run along. Jonah is already way ahead of you."

***

In thirty minutes, the creaking wagon wheels turned in the direction of a safe house that stood among other similar clapboard buildings. Robert jumped from the wagon, proceded up the porch steps and disappeared behind the owner's front door. In short order, he returned and instructed Jonah, "Follow me to the side of the house. A set of steps will take you down into a basement where you'll be met by a dear, sweet widow who'll feed, clothe and help you in any way she can."

As the runaways descended from the wagon, Alex realized he might never see them again. He reached for Jonah's hand and held it firmly. "God bless you, friend, wherever you go. I'll need your prayers, too. The future is uncertain for both of us."

Alex felt Jonah's strong arms embrace him. "We owes you much. Prayers is the most we able to do for you, but we not forget." With that, the group followed their leader into the safe house.

Chapter Twenty

It was two o' clock when Robert and Alex stopped at a three story red brick Victorian home with a multi-colored stained glass window above the front door. Alex's eyes meandered to the side of the house where an airy porch adorned with hanging ferns and comfortable settees beckoned his weary body to rest. A young lady sat reading a book on a swing that resembled the one at Oak Haven. At the sound of shuffling feet, she looked up and scolded, "Father, you're late. What have you been doing? I've baked your favorite pudding."

Robert held out his arms as she rushed to him. "I think you'll forgive me when I tell you we have a guest for lunch, dear. Coreen, this is your cousin, Alex."

For a second, Coreen's strawberry tinted lips parted as she surveyed the stranger, but she offered no words of welcome. Instead, she shied back into her father's arms.

Alex felt his face flush warm with embarrassment, and he realized his appearance shattered any illusions of a 'southern gentleman'. "My apologies for my attire but as I explained to your father, I've had quite an adventure."

The look of distain in Coreen's eyes softened as she stepped forward and offered her hand to Alex. "Forgive my lack of manners. My sister and I have been planning your arrival for weeks. We hope to keep you busy before you head off to fight in this nasty war." She smiled. "Adventure you say. I assure you this family will be all ears."

At Robert's instruction, Henry, a black, male servant, took Alex to a bath house which provided all the necessities to bathe, shave and groom him into a clean gentleman again. A complete set of underwear, stockings, shirt and trousers hung on a wall hanger. As Henry clipped Alex's finger and toe nails, a nagging thought persisted. *Does Uncle Robert have slaves? I'm sure I saw a black woman working over a stove in the kitchen as we passed through the house. Would that not run counter to his uncle's beliefs?* Before he realized it, his thoughts became words. "Henry, did Uncle Robert buy you?"

Henry shook his head and a smile revealed white, even teeth. "No, no, I work as a servant—not a slave. There a big difference. Not like where you come from."

"How's that?"

"My wife, Bessie, and me get paid money to do our job. We savin' to buy us a house of our own. It happen someday. Right now we's happy to be part of this family. Your folk's good people."

"I have much to learn about northern ways, Henry. Right now your wife's cookin' is the first thing on my mind and I expect I've kept everyone waiting long enough."

***

The McPhail girls, Coreen and Jenny, sat at the table and stared in wonder at the amount of food their cousin consumed. Second helpings of vegetable soup, shepherd's pie, bread, pickles, ham, and rice pudding disappeared without a crumb left on Alex's plate.

With a sigh of satisfaction, he placed his napkin on the table, pushed back his chair and smiled at his Aunt Abigail. "Many times at sea I wondered if I'd ever eat a decent meal again after gnawing on hard biscuits and chewing on watered down stew for a month. But this meal has restored my hope. Much obliged, ma'am."

Coreen weighed in before her mother could respond, "I can't wait another minute, Alex. Please tell us all the details of your escapade. Don't leave out a single thing." She put her finger to her lips and instructed, "Now, hush everyone. Listen."

For the next half hour, Alex captured the attention of his relatives and relayed the events as they unfolded day to day. Here and there he embellished a few facts just to see the astonished look on his two cousins' faces and hear their shrieks of excitement.

At the end of his nephew's tale, Robert stood and suggested Alex follow him out to the porch. Once settled on the settee, he pulled a letter from the inside of his jacket and handed it to Alex. "This came a few days ago. While you read it I'll smoke my cigar." He chuckled, "My women don't allow the smoke and aroma past the front door."

"Sounds like a smart move," said Alex as he accepted the letter. At first glance, Sue Ellen's handwriting threatened his resolve, but he fought for control. *No, I'll not cower, no guilt, no going back.* Anxious to read her news, he tore open the envelope and pulled out the lavender-smelling stationery.

Dearest Alex,

There isn't a day goes by that I don't think about you. Your name is lifted up to the Lord in our morning and evening prayers. Everyone is concerned for your well-being. That is, almost everyone. You deserve to know the truth. Father laid down the law at Oak Haven. Your name is never to be spoken under his roof. His rage could be heard from one end of this plantation to the other the day he returned from his trip to Georgia and found you gone. Yes, he brought home breeding hogs and there are litters of piglets meant to grow fat and be slaughtered for the Confederate troops.

I trust for the present you are settled in with Uncle Robert's family. No doubt his girls are making 'much ado' about their handsome cousin with their friends. Enjoy their companionship while you are able. I fear too soon the only excitement you'll see will be on the battlefield.

This may be considered gossip (Andrew will scold me) but I feel you should know that Bella is on the arm of a Confederate officer now. She barely speaks to me at church anymore. I guess as far as you're concerned she believes if you're out of her sight,

then you're out of her mind. In my opinion, no loss, brother.
Joshua and Mammy ask daily if you've written, so please send us a letter soon.
My love forever,
Sue Ellen

Alex felt his jaw muscles tighten with a grimace then a relaxed grin softened the contours of his face. He handed the paper to his uncle through a smoky haze and said, "No secrets. Feel free to read that I'm now a disowned child of Angus McPhail."

"You'll always have a home here, Alex." Robert's voice softened, "My regret is that soon you'll be on the move again. It leaves little time to get acquainted but we'll make the best of it."

"I already feel welcomed into your family, Uncle. The girls are a delight and Aunt Abigail appears to be a kind and sensitive lady who anticipated my needs. I'll never be able to repay you for your kindness."

Robert exhaled the last of the cigar smoke, extinguished the burning stub and changed the subject. "President Lincoln has called for seventy-five thousand volunteers to put down this dispute between the Union and the Confederacy. The general opinion around Boston and Washington is that in a couple months at the most, the whole affair will be history. We outnumber the South in manpower and military equipment. There may be a few skirmishes but in the end the Union will stand. Where do you want to want to serve? Calvary? Infantry?"

Alex did not hesitate. "With my experience in military school the past three years, I believe the Infantry is a better choice. I'm used to drilling and my marksmanship was at the top of the class."

"Well, well, I'm impressed with your credentials." Robert continued, "That tells me where you need to be recruited. I graduated from Harvard and keep in regular contact with alumni and staff. For the past month, the Twentieth Massachusetts Volunteer Infantry, a unit nicknamed the Harvard Regiment, put out the call for men—"

"But Harvard isn't a military institution. Is it not made up of scholars, writers, future politicians and wealthy upper class students? Why would they want to be involved?"

"For the same reason you chose to leave Florida and come fight for the Union. Some of these young men have ancestry that goes back to the forming of the Constitution." Robert sighed as he shook his balding head. "How soon some folks forget we fought a war against an English tyrant for the right to form a nation." His clenched fist came down on the arm of the settee and Alex saw a reddening flush creep up the sides of his uncle's neck. "The providence of Almighty God brought us to this land and I'll do everything in my power to keep it from falling apart."

Chapter Twenty-one

For the next two weeks, a whirl of activity kept Alex involved in the many social affairs orchestrated by his fun-loving cousins. Picnics, tours of the area, rowing on the Charles River and nights spent dancing after sumptuous dinner parties were far removed from his original intention to come north. *I'm on a mission* he reminded himself early one morning. *It's time I put this frivolity behind me and got on with it.*

The smell of freshly brewed coffee led him to the breakfast table where Robert sat reading the morning newspaper. "Well, I didn't expect to see you up at this hour after last evening's celebration. From my observation, our birthday girl had a grand time turning seventeen. I expect there'll be one beau after the other knocking at the door from now on." Robert turned his attention to the front page of the paper and continued, "that is if there's any young men left in Boston. A heavy recruiting campaign to join regiments is well advertised."

"I'm ready to sign up today, sir."

This time Robert folded the paper, looked deep into Alex's eyes. "There's no turning back, son. Are you convinced without a doubt you're making the right decision? I trust any rhetoric you've heard from me hasn't swayed you."

"No cause to worry, Uncle, I made my mind up long before I reached Boston. The Twentieth Massachusetts is where I want to serve. Besides, I'm anxious to see Harvard. Perhaps you can show me around your Alma Mater."

***

An air of excitement met Robert and Alex as they stepped onto the university's campus. Banners and signs posted above the ivy-covered stone walls of that institution read, "Preserve our Union. United we stand. Join the Harvard Regiment."

A sense of pride welled up within Alex and he stepped in line with other young men eager to take an oath of allegiance. The recruitment officer asked his name, age, date of birth, address, occupation, and next of kin. After answering a few medical questions he was given a cursory physical examination and pronounced fit for service.

The sergeant shook his hand and gave him his first order.

"Private, come back in two days, no later than two o'clock, to receive your uniform, boots, canteen, and knapsack. A train will take all new recruits to Camp Massasoit in Readville at three p.m., ten miles away, to start your training. Any questions?"

Alex stood tall and threw back his shoulders. In a crisp voice replied, "No sir. I'm ready to answer President Lincoln's call."

***

Camp Massasoit, under the command of Colonel W. Raymond Lee, sprung up like sprouting mushrooms on the grassy plains near the Neponset River. Row upon row of white canvas tents awaited occupants of multi-ethnic descent. German, Irish, Italian immigrants filled the ranks along with natural-born Americans.

Upon departing the train, the raw recruits formed companies and were escorted to their section of the camp. Alex selected his tent and was pleased to see a rubberized pad lay on a raised wooden platform. A folded wool blanket gave the promise of warmth.

He found delight in unpacking the contents of a basket his aunt passed to him as he left his new home. Inside, he recognized two pair of woolen socks he'd seen her knitting, needles, thread, a pair of scissors, a can of tooth powder, a bar of soap, a brush, comb, and a towel. A box of writing paper, envelopes and a pen reminded him to compose a letter to Sue Ellen after the evening meal. The last item was a tin box. The contents brought a smile to his face as he recognized Bessie's delicious oatmeal cookies he'd smelled baking earlier in the morning.

Alex sat on his makeshift bed and took stock of his surroundings. *No doubt this is as good as it gets. Simple but adequate. No whining, no complaining tolerated here.* The sound of laughter outside his tent interrupted his thought and he opened the flap and saw two young men directly opposite him struggling to erect a collapsed tent.

"I told you to watch out for the pole, brother. These things aren't made of brick you know. Try to steady the center and I'll pull up on the canvas."

Alex sprinted across the grass. One of the two forked stakes had fallen and it left the horizontal ridge pole dangling with the covering ready to collapse.

"Can I be of help?" he asked, grabbing the front stake and holding it steady.

The smaller of the two men pushed straight blond hair away from his eyes and said, "Sure can. Appreciate the help. Not used to maneuvering around a tent. Guess I better get used to it."

A deeper voice took command. "Willie, take hold of the center pole and put it into the notch then we can pull the canvas across. I'll tie the sides down with the twine."

Alex observed the two recruits as they worked to secure their shelter. Although one was smaller and less muscular, they both shared similar facial features—blue eyes, blond hair, high cheekbones, a firm chin and a fair complexion. Handsome lads.

Alex waited until they finished then held out his hand to introduce himself. "I'm Alex McPhail. My tent is opposite yours."

Both men spoke at once. "Thank you for your help." The taller continued, "My name's Hans Baden and this is my brother, Willie. This outdoor living is something we're not used to. Fact is we've got a lot to learn."

"As do I. My former home was nothing like this." Alex surveyed the landscape.

"And where are you from?" asked Willie. "You don't sound as though you're from around here."

"Florida. Close to Tallahassee."

Alex saw an immediate change on both their faces. "But that's in the south," said Hans. "You're wearing a Union uniform."

"And proud to do so. Don't let my southern accent mislead you. I'm not a spy and my roots come from these parts. Let me explain."

For the next ten minutes Alex gave a brief sketch for his reasons to come north then asked, "And why are you volunteering?"

Hans motioned for Alex to sit on the grass beside him.

"We were brought to this country as German immigrants. I was nine years old and Willie eight. Our parents came with a dream to live a life of total freedom. A few months after we arrived, Mother and Father died in a house fire. With no relatives in this land, we were sent to an orphanage. For the past ten years it has been our home, but now that we are considered educated adults, the rules say we must leave and learn to live on our own. The infantry offered a wage plus the opportunity to honor our parents to do our part to continue their dream."

Alex nodded then placed his hand on Hans' shoulder. "Then we have something in common, my friend. My mother died giving birth to me and I was raised by a mammy."

Alex could have sworn he saw a watery glaze form in Willie's eyes before the younger man bowed his head and wiped a hand across the bridge of his nose.

The sound of a dinner bell calling all recruits to the mess hall put an end to any more conversation.

Chapter Twenty-two

Daylight in the northern hemisphere lingered much longer than Alex realized. At 9 p.m., roll call meant he had one more hour before taps—time enough to write Sue Ellen and bring her up to date on his activities. He gathered pen and paper, sat outside and began his letter:

My dear sister,
For the past six weeks, my life has been anything but boring. By pure coincidence the ship I boarded in Jacksonville turned out to be a 'freedom' ship for Negroes. At one point, pirates, eager to confiscate our passengers almost succeeded but a bullet from my revolver killed their leader and the rest surrendered.

If that weren't enough excitement, the night we reached Boston Harbor, vigilantes had the same idea but our captain was one move ahead of them and ordered the Negroes and myself to flee in a skiff to find safety on shore. Thanks to Uncle Robert they are in a 'safe' house which is part of the Underground Railroad.

My heart saddened to hear that I've been disowned by my father but I'm not surprised. Our northern relatives assured me I'm welcome in their home. My cousins have feted me with one delightful activity after another until I decided it was time to live up to my convictions and join the Twentieth Massachusetts Volunteer Infantry. Many of the newer officers are men from Harvard among the higher echelons of society who have little or no military experience, so say an extra prayer for us.

As of today, new recruits are at Camp Massasoit where our commander has the task of training and whipping us into fight-

ing soldiers. Next to my tent are two brothers whom I feel will be true comrades. We expect to be here six weeks so any mail you send, Uncle Robert can deliver. Taps are expected in a few minutes so I'll close for now. All my love,

Alex

Alex dropped his pen and leaned against the tent pole. With his eyes closed, his mind wandered back to the plantation. He visualized cotton opening and the melodic voices of young and old black folk singing spirituals to ease the pain of strained legs and spines. The vision was as clear to him as if he were sitting on the swing at Oak Haven listening to their harmony.

A soft voice brought him back to the present. "Alex, you thinking of your sweetheart? You had a dreamy look on your face and I see you've been penning a letter."

Alex's eyes opened wide and took in his neighbors, Willie and Hans walking toward him.

"Must be tough being so far from her," said the younger brother.

"It's not what you think. I never had a true sweetheart. Now don't get me wrong, my eyes have turned inside out looking at many a pretty Southern gal. Just haven't had the notion I want to settle down yet." Alex waved the paper in the air. "My older sister is waiting to hear all about my trip north. Before they wear us out drilling and parading, I thought I'd ease her curiosity."

Willie, plunked himself on the grass, brought his knees up toward his chin and wrapped slender arms around them. Alex noted an intensity in his new friend's demeanor. "What is life really like in the South? I've never met anyone who came from that part of the country?" A teasing grin crossed Willie's face. "Does everyone sit under huge oak trees fanning themselves drinking mint juleps?"

Alex's chest heaved with laughter. "You've been reading too many romantic stories about us southern folk. Fact is, since the South is an agrarian society, it takes a lot of work to keep up a plantation."

"But the slaves do the work, don't they?"

"Hard labor, yes, but management is the owner's responsibility. My father is constantly checking the quality of the cotton from one end of the fields to the other. Once the bales are ready to market, he negotiates prices with a broker who sees that the cotton is put on a ship to England." Alex sighed and his lips tightened. "Although my father and I have parted company over our political views, I give him credit for his work ethic. It's made him a wealthy man."

"I'm assuming there must be many wealthy families with plantations."

Alex shook his head. "No, most southerners live on small farms with only a handful of slaves, if any at all. A minority of plantation owners own the majority of the richest land and a powerful culture has developed around them. Some folks consider it a closed society."

Willie continued. "Don't you have folks from Europe immigrating to work in the factories—like our parents did? We hear different accents all over Boston. Hans can speak three different languages simply because his friends in our area come from Germany, Italy and even France.

"Well, now that's where we're different. First, there aren't many factories in the south to lure folks from Europe. Remember, the climate is better for farming than it is up here. Besides, most Southerners have their roots either in England, or Scotland. English is the only language I learned. Course some folks up here say they don't always catch what I'm sayin'."

"That's because you talk slow and stretch out your words. Almost like you're not in a hurry to finish what you're saying. Wouldn't hurt us to slow our tongues some. I like your Southern talk, Alex. Don't change your style now that you're part of us."

Alex smiled. He sensed that Hans wanted to weigh into the conversation. "Is it cotton that draws folks to your part of the country? They sure have no experience growing cotton in England. Though they do know a thing or two about farming. I expect the cotton gin fuels the economy and slave labor keeps it going."

"You're right. Cotton is king and it would take a fool to argue it isn't. Think about it. Without the South's cotton all these factories I see up here would become vacant."

"Can't argue with that." Willie started chewing on a fresh blade of grass.

"Doesn't make much sense to me why we have to fight each other."

Politicians in the south have been crying 'States Rights' for some time now." Alex stated. "They believe the Federal government is becoming too strong—not living up to the Constitution."

"And there's a chance the South could lose their slave labor with President Lincoln winning the last election," added Hans. "He's telling the new territories coming into the Union they'll not bring their slaves with them."

The sound of taps brought the discussion to a close. When finished, Alex turned to his friends, "Well, fellas, tomorrow begins our first full day as Union soldiers. Something tells me our lives are never going to be the same."

Chapter Twenty-three

Reveille brought Alex out from under his blanket at 5:30, immediately followed by roll call. After donning his uniform, he pulled on his boots, straightened his bed covering and waited for the company officer to pull back the tent's front flap for an inside inspection. "Private," he announced, "meet me outside in ten minutes."

"Yes, sir."

At the appointed time, one recruit after another stood in a line before their immediate officer as he spoke. "Gentlemen, what I'm about to require of you comes straight from Colonel Lee. He has two priorities for Camp Massasoit—discipline and cleanliness. Our commanders know that disease is as formidable an enemy as the men we are fighting. You've each been given a smallpox vaccination but that is not enough to safeguard your health. The following rules of hygiene will be strictly enforced:

Tents will be aired each morning and weather permitting, every third day, all tents will be struck and bed sacks and blankets turned and exposed to the sunlight. Tent floors are to be swept daily. Food is prohibited within sleeping quarters to avoid attracting rats. Garbage is to be picked up upon sight. Washing days for clothing will be established."

The officer cleared his throat and faced the many eyes focused on him. "The most important requirement of all for controlling human waste is that everyone use the latrine which has been dug at the north edge of the camp. If caught answering nature's call elsewhere, severe punishment will ensue. Is that understood?"

A chorus of 'Yes, sir' echoed through the still morning air.

The last order brought welcomed relief to the troops. "On to breakfast, men."

As a line of blue marched to the kitchen mess halls, Alex listened to some of the independent-minded men render their opinion. "I'll dang well take care of my business wherever it suits. Don't need no greenhorn college officer telling me where to pull my britches down." A string of vulgarity belched from discontented lips.

Another chimed in, "We're here to fight a war, not to spend our time on the other end of a broom."

Alex looked at the rough, muscular, coarse-talking recruits and realized this was in no way like military school. *Somebody's going to have their hands full disciplining this group. Our regiment is doomed for failure if we can't follow orders.*

***

Before the men took to the parade ground for their first lesson in formation drilling, a senior officer had them sit in their designated companies. He unrolled a large cotton sheet that depicted a battlefield and attached it to a wall in the mess hall for all to study. With a long stick, he pointed to illustrated ranks or rows of soldiers. Each man stood side by side with his rifle-musket ready to fire in unison on command. The officer explained, "Even though our weapons have improved since the Revolutionary War, we still believe close ranks are necessary to ensure a massing of continuous firepower that an individual soldier is unable to sustain. Besides, the war departments don't like the idea of wasting ammunition on random targets, although, I'll see to it that you get the opportunity to show off your marksmanship." Satisfaction rippled through the men.

"All right, time to put words into action. For the next two hours you will learn the proper procedures when assembling companies, drilling and marching. Tonight your feet are going to hate you but it's the price you pay for preparing to march twenty, maybe even thirty miles to distant locations. This is the Infantry not the Cavalry. We don't ride horses." A muffled laugh lightened the moment before the senior officer continued, " As you leave with your Company Lieutenant, pick up your new Springfield rifle-musket." The soldiers saw a smug smile cross the officer's face, "If I may boast, your weapon was made right here in Massachusetts. Handle it as though it were your baby and re-member... it may someday save your life."

In a matter of minutes, the mess hall emptied and a ribbon of blue marched to the parade grounds to the beat of a drummer and the shouted commands.

Alex, Hans and Willie fell in together and staked their position along the line.

Each soldier familiarized himself with the left, right and center positions or flanks, as well as the important flag bearer's station. Around and around the parade ground stomped weary men with sweat dripping from their brows. A few collapsed from the heat and had to be carried off the field, but Alex, Willie and Hans maintained their determination to complete the task.

Each confessed later that evening as they sat around a small bonfire nursing their blistered toes that the sight of the Stars and Stripes billowing in the breeze gave them the fortitude to muster on. Removing a foot from a pan of water, Hans sighed, "We made it through the first day and God willing we'll make it through the next...and the next and the next."

But Alex realized as he looked into the faces of his two friends it was more than allegiance to the flag that prompted his resolute will. He sensed a strong bond of brotherhood growing and a sense of personal responsibility for each, especially Willie.

"There's something vulnerable about this young man. I'll be keeping an eye on him."

Chapter Twenty-four

While the following six weeks repeated the same military routine each day, a metamorphous among the troops slowly refined companies of undisciplined, earthy men into soldiers eager to use their military skills. Alex observed another subtle change—one he had never seen before. Autumn. The kaleidoscope of colored leaves that set the trees ablaze never ceased to capture his attention. As they drifted downward from their lofty perch, he collected maple, elm, oak and poplars to send to Sue Ellen. *I can imagine her surprise and delight as she admires their beauty.*

By the time most of the trees stood naked, the opportunity to leave Camp Massasoit came from the newly appointed Army of the Potomac commander, General George McClellan. The official word from command center believed Confederate General Beauregard had plans to make a move against Washington. In preparation, McClellan determined it prudent to keep his army around the capital.

The Twentieth Massachusetts was ready to march. Destination—Camp Benton, in western Maryland situated on sixty acres of land that stretched one mile east of the Potomac River. It offered a wide, level plain that sloped upward to form two small hills. Behind, flowed Broad Run, a small stream with good water. For the time being, this encampment became home for several companies of men. Added to the usual daily drilling, and punctuating the night's stillness, were frequent false alarms. Men aroused from a deep sleep, staggered out of their tents and fell into formation only to march into unknown territory and find no enemy awaiting them.

This scenario changed on October 20 when a scouting party crossed the Potomac River to identify positions of Confederate troops near Leesburg, Virginia. In the dim moonlight an inexperienced leader, Captain Chase Philbrick, mistook a line of trees for tents and reported they had stumbled across an unguarded Confederate camp. Three-hundred men, lead by Col. Devens, crossed the river with orders to attack the camp. To their surprise, upon reaching their destination it became clear there had been a terrible mistake. No such camp ever existed. Rather than withdraw, Col. Devens followed orders and waited for reinforcements to join up with him so they could continue on to Leesburg. These plans were thwarted when pickets from the Seventeenth Mississippi infantry, hidden in the woods spotted Union troops ascending the bluff by way of a trodden cow path. An immediate skirmish ensued. The sound of explosions, the crack of rifles and cries of fighting men prompted the Twentieth Massachusetts to leave nearby Harrison Island in the center of the Potomac for the Virginia side of the river. With only four scows barely able to transport forty men at a time it took three hours to ferry the soldiers across a two-hundred yards of churning water.

By the time Alex, Hans and Willie reached the cleared, flat expanse of ground one-hundred feet above the river, pandemonium reigned everywhere. Smoke from artillery explosions settled like fog obscuring vision, inexperienced soldiers left their formations and ran in all directions, disregarding orders from their superiors. Indiscriminate firing of rifles sent Minie´ balls whizzing through the air, sometimes finding a target but often a waste of ammunition.

Sizing up the situation, Alex shouted to Hans and Willie, "Stay together. We're in a bad situation. The Rebs have the advantage of the woods. We have nowhere to go but over the cliff."

Within minutes, Colonel Baker, leader of the operation, was shot in the head and died instantly. With no one man in command, any resistance the Union troops could muster crumbled and the blood-curdling Rebel yell sent men heading for the river.

"Run for the boats," cried Alex as they clamored over slain

CONVICTIONS

bodies and wailing wounded. In a frenzied scramble, they reached a skiff. Hans lifted Willie and tossed him to the boat's bottom before jumping over the side himself. Just as Alex prepared to do the same, a burly, deep-throated man with an oar threatened to strike him. "No room. We're over-loaded. You'll have to swim."

Alex threw his rifle, hat and jacket to his friends and dove into the river along with several others. At first the shock of the cold water dazed his senses but the sound of Confederate muskets seeking their targets sent him deeper until he could no longer hold his breath. Careful to surface, he took momentary gulps of air before descending again. Since fighting the swift moving current zapped his energy, he let the river decide his course as it swept his body a mile away from the bluff and landed him in the shallows on the far end of the island.

Alex crawled out of the water and collapsed. No longer did he hear gunfire—only the lapping of water against the rocks and fallen water-logged timbers that lay on the shoreline. The serenity of the area compared to the deafening battle sent him into a dreamlike state, and he lay motionless for almost an hour. A resurgence of energy set him on his feet again. *Did Hans and Willie make it across to the island? Did the boat sink? Had a bullet from the enemy struck either one?* His gait grew faster. The sight of smoke from camp fires directed him back to his company. Alex sensed a sullen mood among the men, some wounded, some simply stared out into oblivion, while others cursed the Confederates and even questioned the Union officers' ability to lead.

While searching the remaining troops, Alex heard his name and he ran toward the beckoning voice. In seconds, Willie's arms encircled him. Alex clung to the warmth of the embrace as he realized how close he'd come to death.

Hans came from behind, still holding his friend's belongings. "We thought we'd never see you again. Bullets killed so many swimmers. So sad."

"I learned in Florida how to swim with the current. Without it, I'd never have survived. I ended up on the far end of the island."

Alex lowered his voice but stated the obvious. "I fear poor planning and communication resulted in a badly executed battle today. Many a campfire will not have a full company sitting around it tonight. May their dear souls rest in peace. We owe it to them to learn from our failure and do better."

Chapter Twenty-five

Back at Camp Benton, a lingering sense of discouragement and demoralization had embedded itself in the ranks. The Twentieth Massachusetts could ill afford to lose 204 soldiers either from wounds or death. One of the biggest blows came with the news that their revered leader, Colonel William Raymond Lee, who refused to leave his charges on the river bank was captured and now faced Confederate imprisonment. Hushed murmurs of discontent and accusation circulated around the nightly campfires.

"It's all Captain Philbrick's fault. Inexperience and a know-it-all attitude got us into this battle. Never should have happened. Anyone of us would have checked that site for campfires, pickets, voices."

"Or horses," added another. "Any kind of movement around a bivouac. You's right, he sure wasn't the man for the job."

"Well, let's hope Colonel Palfrey can earn our respect now that he's in command. We got a lot of catchin' up to do if we's gonna beat the Rebs—especially after yesterday's whippin'. Those farm boys know how to shoot. I s'pect they've bin raised with using a firearm long before any of us."

"Course we made our own mistakes," said another. "Saw too many jackets hanging on tree limbs. Might as well have waved a red flag showin' our positions. All bunched up in one area didn't make no sense either. Wouldn't surprise me if we killed some of our own. We're eating humble pie now but we didn't join this fight to lose, so let's make a pact to do better." A chorus of cheers echoed through the night air.

One by one, men drifted away from the campfire and sought rest in their tents. A small group, including Hans, Willie and Alex remained, each lost in their own thoughts as the burning log turn into glowing fragments then disintegrated into gray ash.

One of the troops broke the silence when he announced, "Too bad I don't have a bottle to pass around but I got me some fresh tobacco if anyone wants a chew." He reached into his coat pocket, produced a leather pouch, and handed it to the man next to him.

When it came to Willie, Alex noted his friend hesitated before reaching in and pulling out a small portion of dried, brown leaves. Willie's mouth partially opened and he shoved the wad toward his right cheek. After several chews, his face grimaced and his eyes watered. Suddenly, Willie wretched and spat out the lump of brown foul-smelling tobacco and the remnants of his last meal.

A mocking sneer came from one of the men. "What's the matter, boy? You never chewed before? Ain't 'sposed to swaller the juice. Spit it out." His rant continued, "What's a boy like you doin' here anyway? Somebody outta send you back home. Look fellers, he's still got his baby skin—not a whisker to be seen. This here's a man's war. The infantry's no place for you."

Clenching his hand to his mouth, Willie jumped up and ran into the darkness. Hans followed in quick pursuit.

Back at the campfire, a flash of anger erupted in Alex and he turned to the assailant and said, "Mister, if you ever talk to him like that again, I'll be more than willing to find out how much of a man you are. Willie's not the only young lad in this regiment. It's time you took another look."

Without a word, the soldier stood, spit a stream of tobacco juice in Alex's direction then retreated toward his tent.

For a few minutes, Alex stared into the fading firelight while his racing pulse and ragged breath returned to normal. Jumbled thoughts swirled in his head as he tried to understand his abrupt behavior. *It's not my nature to be confrontational, but there's something about Willie that makes me want to shield him from all the ugliness we face.* He ran his hand through his hair and mentally offered an explanation. *It's in his eyes. They're like magnets drawing me closer, silently begging me to watch over him.*

Alex threw the cold dregs of his coffee onto the dwindling fire and walked to his tent still mulling over his feelings. *Is it my business to get involved in protecting Willie when he has a big brother? Why am I so concerned about a fellow comrade?*

As he tossed and turned on his mat, these questions followed him into a confusing dream where images of his relationships with former girlfriends, his sister, Sue Ellen, and even the slave girls melded into one face with blond hair and smokey-blue eyes. No, it can't be. I refuse to believe it. Finally, his neighbor's features faded into oblivion as sleep erased disturbing thoughts.

***

Although the calendar indicated the fall season, Indian Summer, blessed the troops with, warm, hazy sunny days. The men took advantage of the pleasant weather and worked hard on their drilling skills. By evening they were tired, sweaty and hungry.

Over the weeks at Camp Benton, each company took turns at night picketing. After a day of rigorous activity, the shift was usually one of boredom and exhaustion. Alex fought fatigue by looking forward to riding through the woods and valleys on one of the company's horses. He missed his daily habit of exercising Starlight and hoped Joshua had taken his place.

On the third evening of his picket, he rode his horse over the level ground away from the tents, up an incline and into the woods beside the stream. Sensing his horse's need of water he led the grey mare slowly in that direction. Always aware of unusual noises while on duty, his ears perked up at the sound of a splash in the trickling stream. He reached for his revolver and approached with caution as his eyes adjusted to the dwindling light. Circular ripples fractured the water indicating movement.

Is it a beaver, a fish, a human?

Within seconds, Alex saw a naked female with small protruding breasts, a curved narrow waist with slender hips and thin shapely legs break the surface. Her eye lids remained closed as droplets of water glistened on her porcelain skin.

Transfixed on the sight before him, Alex struggled for his next breath. *Am I seeing things?*

Suddenly the braying of the horse caught her attention and smokey-blue eyes popped open.

"A-A-Alex," she stammered then sank to her knees to cover her nakedness."

"Willie? You ARE a ..." He turned away before finishing, "woman!"

Relief washed away the confusion Alex had felt for months. Now he understood her refusal to use the company latrine, her skill in using a needle and thread when it came to replacing missing jacket buttons, and her awkward movements when climbing over fallen obstacles when on the march. It especially explained his feelings of protection and yes, even attraction toward her.

A trembling voice responded, "Please, don't move. Let me dress, I'm freezing. I can explain." Willie rushed to the shore and grabbed her clothing from a hanging branch. In less than a minute she said, "I'm ready to confess."

Alex noted how the uniform covered any trace of a female and Willie once again became Private Baden. Before he uttered a word, she pleaded, "Please don't turn me in." Tears ran down her reddening cheeks. "I won't leave my brother. He's all I've got and nowhere to go. I can do this; other women are in disguise, too. I proved myself on the battlefield. I can do the drills and the marching. Please, Alex, let me stay." Alex shook his head and tried to reason with a soldier he'd grown to respect.

"But you can die—you're too young. I'd never forgive myself if a bullet or a cannon blast took your life. And how would Hans feel? I can't believe he let you away with this foolishness."

"He didn't know. I waited until he enlisted and a few days later showed up at the camp. I lied and told them we were cousins. It's something I have to do. No different than you. You broke from your father and followed your heart."

She's right, he conceded. *I can't dispute her argument as much as it makes no sense.* Alex took a deep breath and looked into her pleading eyes. "This is crazy; for now I'll keep your secret but if things get really rough, and my instinct tells me it will, I'll be the first one to send you away."

Alex saw relief replace the fear on her face as she wiped away the tears. She reached up and grabbed his hand, squeezing it with all her might. "Thank you. You'll be proud of me. Just one more thing…"

Alex felt the release of her hand. "And what would that be?"

"Continue to call me Willie and act as though I'm male. It could be easy to slip and the others may not be so compassionate."

A smile preceded Alex's tease. "You have my word. Now jump up behind me. That's an order. I'm taking you back to the edge of the field. You disobeyed by leaving the bivouac, soldier."

"Yes, sir."

As she wrapped her arms around his waist, Alex felt in his heart a new chapter in his life was on the horizon.

Chapter Twenty-six

Alex could not erase the memory of his encounter with Willie at the stream. He tossed and turned all night, and by morning the sound of reveille grated on his nerves. Drained of energy, he threw back his blanket and went through the motions of the daily inspection routine. All the while, he fought a mental battle. *Did I do the right thing? Should I go back on my word and turn her in? Is it possible for a woman to survive the physical demands of war? And what about the environment itself with vulgar-talking, coarse-mannered males physically strong compared to her limited strength? Hans and I need to talk.*

The opportunity presented itself during an afternoon break from musket drill maneuvers. While instructed to clean their rifles, the two sat side by side away from any eavesdroppers. At first each concentrated on the task at hand. Neither spoke and Alex felt an uncomfortable silence between them. *Can I tell him how I discovered Willie's secret? Maybe he knows? Will he believe I never touched her?* His tongue felt twice its size and any saliva in his mouth evaporated. After juggling words around in his mind he blurted, "Hans, I have a confession. Last night I..."

"Alex, it's all right. My sister told me what happened. I'm just thankful it was you who found her. I shudder to think of the outcome had it been any other man in our company. You're a true southern gentleman. You have my wholehearted respect."

Alex sighed with relief. "She took a huge chance, Hans."

"I know and I've reprimanded Willie for her behavior. She's an independent woman with a mind of her own. I even threatened to turn her in if she tries a trick like that again."

"Perhaps you should for her own safety."

"I've tried to reason with her but in a strange way, despite the danger, I understand why she's here. I've told you our background. When the only thing we've got in this world is each other, how can I let her go?"

"I understand. It was hard leaving my sister," Alex softened his tone, "never knowing if we'd ever meet again. Your sister can be very persuasive," Alex said smiling, " especially when you look into those big blue eyes."

"Ahh, so you've noticed." Hans grew serious. "I actually feel relieved that you discovered her charade. Maybe between the two of us we can shield her from harm. But take my advice—don't let her know you've got her in your sights. She thinks she can handle herself."

Alex chuckled, "We'll see about that, now won't we."

***

As the days grew shorter and the nights colder, it was no surprise that one cloudy night Mother Nature blanketed Camp Benton with two inches of pristine snow. Whoops and hollers outdid the call of the bugle as men woke to a complete change of scenery. Naked branches, covered in white, glistened as rays from a rising sun bounced from one to another. To Alex, the ground resembled a full field of blossoming cotton without the pickers. To others, it was fodder for hard-packed snowballs that whizzed through the air reaching some innocent victim.

Even though the following winter months presented a reprieve from actual combat, it brought something else the men fought daily—boredom. Continued drills and marches into the same familiar territory took up several hours in a day but when maneuvers finished, it was up to the troops to develop ways to amuse themselves. Alex, among many others, wrote letters, read their Bibles, newspapers, and books.

Cunning card and checkers players often tried to cheat their opponent out of a portion of a month's meager pay. A flash of temper usually ended up in a squabble with fists flying in all directions. More than once Alex stepped in to subdue the commotion before an officer broke up the brawl.

Restless men craved physical activity during these months of calmness. Boxing, foot racing, and wrestling became popular sports. Competition among different companies demanded a wager, whether it be money, a week's supply of coffee, tobacco or a pair of extra socks.

While sitting around a fire one evening, one of Company A's enthusiast announced, "Hey, boys, those Irish lads in Company C are itchin' to take us on in a wrestlin' match after drill tomorrow. What d'ya say? Show 'em what were made of." A shout of agreement from the majority sealed the deal.

The ring leader walked over to Willie. "We'll start with you. They've got a lad or two your size. I bet once you strip off that coat you're a real tiger."

Alex saw the sudden fear in Willie's eyes as she stammered, "I never wrestled nobody. Don't know how."

"Ah, you can do it. Just pretend it's a Johnnie Reb."

"Yeah," echoed several sitting in the group.

Alex rushed in, "Nah, let me start the bout." He pointed at Willie. " Ain't no muscle on that scrawny skeleton. We want to win don't we?"

Several heads nodded. "Well then, it's settled. I can't wait to put a head-lock on some poor geezer. If any of you are bettin' men, I won't disappoint you. For now, it looks like it's best if I get a good night's sleep. See y'all in the morning."

Alex made his way back to his tent and prepared to settle in for the night when he heard a familiar voice whisper his name. "Alex, may I come in?"

"Willie, is something wrong? What do you want?"

A sliver of moonlight fell on the right side of her face enhancing the sculptured cheekbones and brightened the gold in her hair.

"You volunteered on purpose to save me from wrestling, didn't you?" She moved closer.

"Well, I suppose I did. It would have blown your cover and besides I didn't want to see you hurt. Those guys play for real."

"It's not the men I'm afraid of." She lay her hand on his. "I owe you a debt I'll probably never be able to repay. Thank you. Your mammy raised you right. You saw I was heading for trouble and came to my rescue. Now you have to face some fightin' Irishman. Rest assured there'll be an extra prayer whispered on your behalf tonight." Alex felt the squeeze of her hand as she turned and walked back to her tent. He smiled in the darkness. *You needn't worry, little lady. These Irish are in for a surprise. Joshua and I spent many a day tussling and sparing. Wrestling is no stranger to me.*

Chapter Twenty-seven

The following day Mother Nature had plans of her own. A blinding blizzard swept through the camp leaving eight inches of snow, canceling any suggestion of a wrestling match. As evening approached and the winds died down, a peaceful hush settled over the encampment. Intermittent snowflakes drifted from the sky and added to the accumulation.

Alex, Hans and Willie huddled together in the larger tent each wrapped in a woolen blanket sipping hot coffee. Out of the stillness the sound of a lone fiddle began to play 'Swing Low Sweet Chariot'. Seconds later a flute joined in and following their lead a harmonica. Together a sweet, soulful melody wafted through the plunging frigid air. A repertoire of music, some lively, some subdued, touched a hidden emotion deep within Alex's heart and a wave of homesickness brought tears to his eyes. A sniffle from his reddening nose caught his friends' attention and he noticed their look of concern.

"You okay, Alex? The cold hasn't made you sick has it?" asked Hans.

Embarrassed, he expressed his feelings. "No, no, I'm not sick. The music takes me home to Oak Haven. In the evenings we used to sit on the front porch and listen to the Negroes harmonize as they sang their spirituals." Alex wiped a tear from his cold cheek. "Just goes to show you that God's music is universal."

"Trouble is," cut in Willie, "wars aren't won with music. The boom of the cannon drowns out any hope of that."

***

It was well after midnight when Alex woke with chills racing through his body followed by a surge of heat that produced beads of sweat on his brow. Fever. For the past two weeks sickness ran rampant through the ranks, forcing men to lie low. It was no surprise. Sleeping on wooden platforms four inches above the frozen ground was not only uncomfortable but lacking in adequate warmth. It took every bit of Alex's energy to keep from freezing. By morning, his bones ached and he had difficulty moving his limbs. When he did not respond to roll call, the sergeant entered his tent and demanded a response.

"I'm ill, sir. Came on suddenly in the night. Can't seem to move a muscle."

The officer scrutinized Alex then gave an order. " Looks to me like swamp fever. It's all over the camp—spreads fast, too. No use sending you to the doctors; they'll give you the same advice I've heard all week. Stay confined to your tent and drink lots of liquids. Should pass in a couple days. I'll have the fellas next door bring you some grub."

"Thank you, sir." Alex pulled the blanket tighter around his shoulders and tried to go to sleep.

***

"But we've got to keep his body warm, Hans," urged Willie. "I have an idea. Remember at the orphanage when that awful flu spread through the town. Folks used this old tactic to keep their families from dying. Stones—heated stones placed next to a body to ward off the chills."

"I do remember. It's not going to be easy huntin' them under all this snow." Willie pointed to a field near the woods. "Over by that maple tree there's a pile that some farmer must have pulled while readying this land for sowing. Go. See what you can find. I'll start the fire." As she watched her brother trudge through the snow she could not help but proclaim, "Don't you dare die on me, Alex McPhail. I won't let you."

All day, Hans and Willie continued to wrap heated slabs of

stone in burlap and place them under Alex's blanket. At times he was oblivious to the activity around him and teetered on the edge of delirium calling out to Mammy to bring him water. At each request, Willie placed her friend's canteen against dry, swollen lips and urged him to drink.

After many hours and Hans' insistence, the company doctor stopped on his rounds to check on Alex's condition. Hans and Willie saw the solemn expression on the man's face as he placed an experienced hand on the young soldier's brow. He put his ear close to Alex's nose and mouth to analyze his breathing. He discovered it was shallow and intermittent.

The doctor turned to Hans and said, "If he lives 't'ill morning he'll be a lucky lad. I've pronounced three dead today and I've no reason to believe there won't be more tomorrow. Men behind the shovels have been busy— especially since the ground is frozen." The man stood up and Willie and Hans saw a glint of hope cross his weary face. " Good idea using the heated stones. Keep him warm and offer him water as often as he'll take it. There's a chance he might beat the odds. One thing's for sure…"

"What's that?" cut in Willie.

"This one is blessed to have you two caring for him." The doctor's voice trembled, "so many are left to die alone."

Chapter Twenty-eight

Daylight erased the darkness inside Alex's tent while a soft, nasal purr caught his attention. He opened his eyes to discover strands of disheveled blonde hair partially covering a familiar face sleeping beside him. *Willie? Why is she here?*

Before his mind had time to fathom the situation, Hans threw open the tent flap and gasped, "Thank God. I half expected to see a corpse. We had little hope you'd survive the fever. The doctor told us others haven't been so lucky."

"I'm more than lucky. Looks as though the two of you spent the night caring for me. I felt the fever break about three o'clock." Alex turned toward Willie and lowered his voice. "She wore herself out, didn't she?"

"Refused to leave your side. Insisted the warm stones would force you to sweat it out. Looks as though she was right."

Hans gently shook his sister's shoulder. "Hate to wake her up but bugle call's about to blast and she doesn't need to be seen coming out of your tent."

A sly grin creased the edges of Alex's lips. "If this company only knew who slept here last night the ole grapevine would be buzzin' this morning. See you at breakfast—can't wait to sink my teeth into more of that hardtack."

***

A walk to the sutler's wagon put some energy back into Alex's mental and physical body. Since the mail system between the North and South no longer existed, he felt starved for news beyond his regiment's bivouac and the sutler always brought a bountiful supply of newspapers. He couldn't wait to return to his tent and devour every word before he passed it on to his comrades.

The headline, in large black, bold print caught his attention the moment Alex opened the paper. **Prisoner exchange: Colonel William Lee to Return to the 20th Massachusetts**

For a moment, he thought his eyes deceived him and he read it again. Instant elation stirred his emotions. *Finally, some good news, a glint of hope to ignite the morale of our troops. Lieutenant Colonel Frank Palfrey, with his slothful ways has done nothing but divide the unity of this regiment with his political and ethnic factions. But how did this miracle come about?*

Alex searched the front page of the newspaper for the facts which he mentally summarized into a brief explanation in order to spread the news. According to the article, the Schooner, Savannah, was captured coming out of Charleston Harbor. Its fourteen member crew, now in irons, sailed on a Union ship to New York to be tried as pirates and later to be hung.

In Libby prison, where Colonel Lee was in confinement, thirteen Union officers of highest rank were chosen by lot to be hung in retaliation by the Confederates. In the end, calmer heads prevailed, and a prisoner exchange checked the thirst for blood.

Alex gained a new layer of respect for Colonel Lee as the paper quoted him: "I left home thinking it possible that I might die on a battlefield, but if my country thinks that I can serve best by dying at the hangman's hands, I can meet even that death without a shudder." *

Leaving the rest of the newspaper to be read later, Alex chose the front page and hustled outside shouting, "Colonel Lee's is free to come back. It's in the paper."

A small group of German troops preparing a campfire yelled back, "What'd you say? Something about Lee?"

Alex pointed to the headline. "Here, read it yourselves."

Within seconds their native tongue bellowed a chorus of

"Hurra!" three times.

"Not a minute too soon if you ask me," offered a soldier placing a hunk of firewood on an ignited oak limb. "If Palfrey doesn't stop with his unfair promotions, he'll ruin this regiment."

Another piped up. "Not only that, he's got the abolition folk divided against those that believe they're stickin' their neck out to preserve the Union. No way to prepare for battle if you ask me. The troops are soon gonna' wonder who's the enemy? Confederates or the Twentieth Massachusetts fightin' among ourselves."

***

By the middle of March, President Lincoln, tired of McClellan's delays, directed the general to reorganize the Army of the Potomac into four corps in preparation to invade peninsular Virginia and head west toward Richmond. When Colonel Lee returned to the regiment in May, he found a different regiment then the one he'd known before his capture. With many of the original officers either killed or gone, a new slate of commanders were in control. The troops were warned that the fiasco at Ball's Bluff had been but one day of battle, where as this new development into Virginia was a campaign that could last months.

While striking their tents on the day of departure, Alex kept looking at Willie as she packed her knapsacks with clothing and personal items. *She shouldn't be doing this. Up to now our soldiering has been bearable, even for a woman, but when we march miles on end enduring all kinds of weather, constant battle anxiety or even food shortages, how will she survive?* With each negative thought he could stand it no longer and walked to her side. With his head bent low he spoke in a hushed tone. "Come with me. We need to talk."

He saw her puzzled look before she put down her canteen and followed him away from the others and into the edge of the woods. With no one to hear them, Alex stated his concern, but he soon realized as he stared into determined eyes and a rigid stance that he argued in vain.

"Willie, turn yourself in. I beg you. This past year has been a picnic compared to what the future may hold. Think of the burden it puts on your brother trying to protect you and I must admit as a southern bred gentleman, I feel a responsibility for your safety, too. Any man with sensibility wouldn't encourage a woman to go to war."

Willie put her hands on her hips and stretched her five- foot-five frame to its fullest extent before she spoke, "If I fall to the wayside and die from fatigue, Alex McPhail, it would have been worth every step my aching feet have taken." Her flushed cheeks and defiant tone signaled to Alex he struck a nerve. "I'm part of this army and I intend to give it all I've got. Now, let's put an end to this condescending conversation and get back to the business of departure. Or do you intend to be the last to leave?" With her head held high she threw back her shoulders and marched back to the camp leaving Alex shaking his head in defeat.

***

With four days rations tucked away in their haversacks, the Twentieth Massachusetts left the winter quarters and started their journey. They marched overland until they reached the Potomac River. Here they boarded schooners, sailed down the river then south to Chesapeake Bay over to Fort Monroe at Hampton.

Eager to reach Virginia's capital, the troops soon realized that General McClellan was hesitant to engage the enemy. Unsubstantiated reports that the Confederates troops outnumbered the Union's held the general back, but it kept the men on edge.

"He must be afraid the Rebs will whip us. What's he waiting for?" groaned one man after another. "We came here to fight—not crawl along like worms after a rain. How long we gonna' be pluggin' through these swamps knee-deep in water and mud?"

It was on one of these days that Willie faced an enemy of Nature as ominous as any Reb. A torrential downpour produced flooding conditions that spread a watery grave for much of the wildlife living throughout the flat surface. Animals and reptiles scurried up tree trunks, branches and stumps of rotting logs seeking shelter.

Following between Hans and Alex, sloshing through knee-high water, Willie carried her rifle above her head in order to keep it dry. Suddenly, she felt the fangs of a reptile strike exposed skin on her left arm. She screamed as her rifle dropped from her hand into the murky water. In seconds Hans slashed the snake's body in half with his bayonet while Alex ripped fangs from her bleeding flesh.

He thrust his cap into her mouth and ordered, "Bite as hard as you can. This is going to hurt. I've got to cut an X on your arm and suck out the venom. We can't let it get into your bloodstream." One hand lifted her chin and he looked into scared, tearing eyes. "You can do this, Willie. Hans, get behind and hold her steady."

With his Bowie knife in hand, Alex took a deep breath and cut the incision. He felt Willie's body flinch then go weak as she fainted. With trembling lips, Alex placed them on the flowing blood and sucked until his mouth was full then spat it out. He repeated this procedure several times until he felt he captured as much venom as possible.

Hans looked into his sister's face. The pallor on her skin sent a chill through his burly body and he picked her up in his arms. "I'll carry her. A sack of flour weighs more than her."

Alex squeezed his friend's arm. "We'll take turns. Could be miles before we're ordered to stop."

After several minutes, Willie came to and started to squirm in protest. "Let me down. I don't need to be carried." With one huge effort to separate herself from her brother's muscled arms, she realized her weakness and fell against his shoulder.

Alex saw the frustration she bore and he calmed her down with words of advice. "You need to be still, Willie. The more agitated your movements, the easier it is for the poison to travel through your body. Keep your arm down below your heart. It won't be long now before we reach the bivouac. I can see camp fires on up ahead."

The dwindling daylight soon gave way to giant shadows cast by the enormous pine trees surrounding multitudes of hastily erected tents. Willie lay on a bed of pine straw while the two closest men in her life secured her sleeping quarters.

Once in the tent, she watched as Alex scavenged inside his haversack, drew out a spool of white cotton material, cut off a length and soaked it with water from his canteen. Before he proceeded to cleanse the oozing wound, he yelled to Hans, "Strike up a fire and get the coffee on. I'll tend to the patient."

His gentle touch soothed Willie's nerves and in a soft whisper she said, "You've probably saved my life."

"And you mine—remember. A cold winter night. Hot stones." A gentle voice chuckled, "So now we're even."

A moment of silence passed between them and Willie closed tired eyes. As she drifted off to sleep, Alex pushed back strands of unruly hair that fell against her nose. He softly brushed his lips against her forehead. An unfamiliar quiver sent warm tentacles throughout his body. He savored the moment. *She must survive. My heart tells me she must.*

Outside, Alex moved close to Hans and lowered his voice. "Check her arm tonight for swelling. If the wound changes color and red streaks run up her arm, she's in trouble. Blood poisoning."

Stoking the fire, Hans asked, "How is it you know so much about snake bites?"

Alex drew in a deep breath. "Never had one myself but I saw many a slave get bitten. The rattlesnakes in Florida coil up under the cotton plants for shade. They get a might nasty when struck by a hoe. My friend Joshua got bit one time and Mammy showed me what to do. It works if done quick enough."

Han's voice trembled, "Did anyone on your plantation ever die from a snake bite?"

Alex heard the fear and placed an arm around Hans's shoulder. "Honestly, yes, but we reacted quickly and that's half the battle."

CONVICTIONS

"What's the other half?"
"Are you a praying man, Hans?"
"Not like I should. Mama tried to teach me."
"Well, tonight my friend would be a good time to start again."

*(Harvard's Civil War/Richard F. Miller)

Chapter Twenty-Nine

To the soldiers' relief, two weeks later, General McClellan called for a day of rest from the continuous lumbering through mud, swamps and hordes of blood-sucking mosquitoes. After several days of continuous rain, the clouds scattered and gave way for the warmth of the sun. Hastily erected clotheslines soon filled with underwear, socks, shirts, trousers and coats in order to dry out before pellets of water soaked them again.

Alex noted that an elevated, positive mood among the troops often followed a change in the weather. Less whining—more laughter. His own spirits rose with the sight of Willie chasing after Hans with her left arm flailing a stick in the air.

Looks like she's back to normal. No signs of poisoning. Thank God I listened and watched one of your survival lessons, Mammy.

The thought of this dear, sweet woman brought a smile to his face and he reached inside a breast pocket and pulled out two letters he'd received from the mail courier, settled back on his mat and read:

Dear Alex,

I follow your travels by way of the newspaper and I can assure you your name is brought forth in our home continuously. The girls keep asking when the war will be over and I must admit, I have no answer. According to sources, General McClellan's lack of initiative and inability to plan efficiently has President Lincoln in a state of frustration and I fear the man may not be leader of the Army of the Potomac much longer.

I've pondered your disappointment over cancelled mail serv-

ice between Union and Confederate states. Although I understand letters could jeopardize the security of our troops if locations and other secrets were openly disclosed, it has to be difficult being cut off from Sue Ellen and news from the South.

My freedman, Henry, came up with a solution. Since he's an abolitionist, he travels into the Confederate states helping fugitive slaves find their way north through the Underground Railroad. I instructed him a month ago to travel to Florida and locate Oak Haven. I'm delighted to inform you that he met with your sister and brought back the enclosed letter she has written to you.

Alex felt excitement generate in the pit of his stomach and he picked up the lavender smelling envelope addressed to him. Oh, yes, this is my sister's handwriting and favorite scent. Before opening it, he continued to read Robert's letter.

Please, write when you're able and do not hesitate to ask for anything you need. May our Almighty God favor you and our troops with victory soon.

Uncle Robert

While Alex pulled his second letter from the envelope, Willie appeared at the tent's opening, her face pink from the afternoon sun. "Come play a game of horse shoes with us. We need one more body for a team."

Alex motioned for her to sit beside him and he waved Sue Ellen's letter in the air. "Willie, I've received the most amazing news—a letter from my sister. It's been over a year since I last heard from her."

Willie snuggled close and drew in a long breath. "Ah, lavender. What a wonderful smell. I'm so tired of inhaling open latrines." She reached for the envelope. "Let me smell it again."

Alex smiled at her feminine side and handed it to her. "Keep it. The letter's the important part."

Willie started to rise. "Meet us at the parade ground. I'll let you read in private."

Alex reached out and caught her arm. "No need to leave." His voice grew softer. "I'd really like to share it with…a friend."

CONVICTIONS

Willie sat down and watched as Alex unfolded the stationary. A group photo of Sue Ellen, Andrew, Joshua, and Mammy fell on the ground. He picked it up and stared into each face. A lump caught in his throat and his eyes watered. *Had it been almost two years since he'd waved good-bye?* He handed the photo to Willie and said, "My family. Father no doubt refused to sit for his son." The corners of Alex's mouth fell but Willie nudged his arm and said, "I'm listening, read."

Dearest brother,

How fortunate we are to have an uncle who cares that we keep in contact. I've been in complete despair knowing the mail service cut off any news from you. Henry assured me that you are well and still eager to serve the Union.

I now have two men in my life who keep my prayer life active. Andrew accepted Jefferson Davis's call for volunteers after seeing the desperate need for more men to serve in the infantry six months ago. The last correspondence from my dear husband came from Virginia, where as you know, the majority of the fighting has been. I miss him terribly and poor Mammy is worn out trying to keep my spirits positive.

Joshua has been such a help around the plantation and continues to study the books I encourage him to read. He wants you to know that even though you are fighting in a war, he can still wrestle you to the ground and looks forward to the day he can prove it.

Father's stance on political issues remains resolute. I do believe he expected the South to wrap up this disagreement months ago so his temperament is volatile and we stay out of his way. I see signs of aging in his walk and facial features. Of course his whiskey drinking habits have not abated and in fact he spends more and more time with old friends passing around a bottle.

Florida has been spared major battles and Union soldiers are not trampling down our soil and pillaging our food supply as we hear they do in other states. Of course cotton bales sit in the fields yielding no income so that's an irritation for Father, too.

I try not to complain as I'm well aware that many other women are suffering much more than I. Deep down in my heart I know the life you and I knew growing up is lost forever. How we adapt to the changes is a challenge each of us will face.

Well, I must not keep Henry waiting so I'll close this letter with prayers and an everlasting love for you.

Sue Ellen

Willie watched Alex fold the letter with care and place it in his Bible. She wiped away a tear before she said, "Your sister sounds like a wonderful person. I suspect the both of you are much alike—kind, smart, respectful."

Without hesitation, Alex held up his hand as if in denial. "Nah, not me. I've got a long way to go before I catch up to her."

Willie saw the blush of modesty deepen the color in his cheeks and she continued her accolade. "There's something different about you Alex. You stand apart from the rest of the men in this company." As she prepared to leave, Willie turned and teased. "And I intend to find out what it is."

Chapter Thirty

To the troops of the Twentieth Massachusetts, the summer of '62 dragged on. Occasionally drills were held but the regiment spent the majority of its time doing work detail, laying logs across swampy areas to construct make-shift roads, building bridges or pulling loaded wagons and horses out of the continuous muck. A rotating picket schedule of twenty-four hours every three days for each unit brought out fear, uncertainty and criticism in those ordered to put themselves in danger.

"Why don't McClellan order us to charge and get it over with instead of some Johnny Reb pickin' us off one man at a time. Being out there on picket duty is spooky, not knowin' if someone's got a bead on ya," complained many a soldier.

As one scorching month after another turned into fall, it was obvious to those in the Infantry that McClellan's strategy to capture Richmond by getting between Confederate General Joseph E. Johnston and the Capital, showed signs of unraveling. The continuous appeal from McClellan for reinforcements fell on deaf ears and the help he counted on from the Union ships in the James and York rivers never materialized since the iron-clad Confederate Virginia ship blocked their way.

With pressure from the President to 'make a move', McClellan finally approached Yorktown with caution, but to his surprise the foe had evacuated. Still, he pressed on, confronted with burned bridges, heat, fatigue, a scarcity of rations, and skirmishes that gained little.

During the battle at Fair Oaks, Colonel Johnston, wounded, left the field. The following day he was replaced by General

Robert E. Lee, who took a more offensive attitude toward the Army of the Potomac. For seven days he hammered his foe at every opportunity until McClellan realized Richmond was a lost cause and he gave the command to retreat. Troop morale plummeted.

It was during the week's last battle that Willie suffered a war-weary breakdown. Nauseated by artillery smoke, confusion, terrific noise from exploding shells and whistling Minie´ balls, she wandered away from her scattered company and into a wooded area. The late afternoon sun produced eerie shadows that in her mind resembled lurking Confederate soldiers.

Along with this thought, a sickening, paralyzing fear gripped her body at the words, "Halt!" For a few seconds her feet froze. She stood immobile until a deep, guttural sound once again commanded, "Turn around and look at me. I want to see your Yankee face take one last breath before I pull the trigger."

Willie tightened her grip on her rifle and slowly turned toward a bearded man whose black eyes bored into hers. A twisted, evil smirk on his dirt-smudged face sent the adrenalin pounding in her veins. *He's going to kill me. Please, Lord, help me.*

"Yes, sir-ee, I got me a young Yankee. Should have stayed home, boy."

By now, Willie felt every beat of her heart and breathing became difficult. Her eyes never wavered from the approaching foe—one step closer; another step closer. He raised his gun and took aim. She heard the click of the hammer. With a final step his foot caught on an exposed tree root, he stumbled forward and the shot went wild. Hers did not. In a split second, she pulled the trigger on her Springfield and the man fell to the ground. Blood gushed like a fountain from his left temple. His lifeless body sent shock waves through Willie and she began to shake uncontrollably. *I've got to get out of here.* Tears blinded her vision as she tried to get her bearings. With her free left hand she wiped away the wetness and looked to the sun for direction. A sinking ball in the west indicated she needed to continue walking south to the camp site.

CONVICTIONS

Meanwhile, Hans and Alex returned to their tents within minutes of each other. Alex no sooner put down his gun and canteen when he heard Hans calling, "Alex, did you see Willie? She should be here by now."

"She was following you. After the order was given to fall back, I know I saw her a few yards behind you."

Panic gripped Han's response. "She never leaves us. Suppose she's been hit, captured, or lost." Hans ran for his gun. "I'm going to find her."

"Not without me, friend." Alex grabbed his revolver and lantern.

The two men retraced their steps into the battlefield. There was just enough light to see mangled, human carnage scattered among the weeds and grass. Several times they almost tripped on a stiffening body.

Alex stopped and surveyed the rectangular field. Not another living soul did he see until movement caught his eye at the edge of the woods. A lone figure meandered as though walking in a zig-zag pattern. He motioned to Hans to get low. "It could be a Reb on picket duty. Crawl if we have too."

The two crept closer until they both recognized a blue uniform. Blonde hair peeked out from under the cap. That was enough proof for Hans and he broke into a run toward his sister. A warm embrace followed as Alex caught up to them.

"I... killed... a man." Willie's words came out in short quips as tears streamed down her face. "I shot him in the head. He was going to shoot me." Every inch of her body trembled. "I'm a killer. I've taken a man's life."

Alex stepped forward and cupped her face in his hands. "Willie, we're in a war. That's what happens in war. You know that. This isn't the first battle you've fought."

"But this was different. More personal. Before, when I shot my rifle with everyone else, I never really knew if I hit anyone." She shivered again. "He came up behind me. I never heard him until it was too late. He wanted to see me die. Told me so. I'll never forget his evil face." With that she broke down and sobbed while

Alex gathered her into his arms and tried to soothe her trembling body.

Hans got her moving. "C'mon, we can't stand out in the open with pickets in the woods. "I'll take the lead back to camp. No wanderin' off, Willie. We don't want to lose you again."

***

After a portion of fried hardtack and a cup of coffee, Willie explained how the poor visibility got her off track and she walked into the sniper's trap. Again, Alex tried to convince her that she acted in self defense and no guilt feelings were warranted.

Exhaustion sent all three to their mats as a full moon climbed high above touching the earth with a silver glow. Sometime during the night, Alex awoke to the sound of soft crying outside his tent. He pulled back the front flap and sitting in the moon's light was Willie with her head bowed and her shoulders drooped. Not wanting to alarm her by his presence or take the chance of waking those sleeping nearby, he stayed put and softly called, "Willie, it's Alex, what's wrong?"

She jerked her head up and wiped her eyes with the back of her sleeve. "I woke you. So sorry."

Alex took a few steps, sat beside her then took her hand in his. "It's about killing that man, isn't it?"

She nodded before she spoke. "I can't get to sleep. All I can see is his ugly face and determined look in his evil eyes. Oh, Alex, one part of me says turn myself in and flee from this hell, but another cries, 'You're strong; you can do this. Don't give in to the enemy.' Besides," she squeezed his hand, "how can I leave you and Hans?"

Alex looked into her pleading face and made a decision. "C'mon, you're spending the rest of the night with me. Tomorrow's another day and there's no tellin' where we'll be marching or for how long." He stood and pulled her up off the ground and into his tent.

"We can share my mat. Every time that horrible vision threatens to rob your sleep, squeeze my arm to remind you I'll never let anyone hurt you."

Willie settled her body next to Alex and they lay together like a pair of spoons. Within five minutes, Alex heard her breathing change from irregular gulps of air to a mellow, soft rhythmic pattern. As he felt her rigid limbs melt into a relaxed position, he sighed, *This could be the best sleep I've had in months.*

Chapter Thirty-one

While McClellan's forces retreated from the Virginia Peninsular battle fields, General Robert E. Lee, motivated by success during the Seven Days Siege, took the initiative to leave Virginia and take the fight to the Union's home ground. After victory over Major General John Pope at the Second Battle of Manassas, he led his army across the Potomac River and settled near the town of Sharpsburg, Maryland. There the troops indulged in autumn's harvest of much needed food supplies. Fresh fruits and vegetables filled the bellies of starving soldiers.

Having read the northern newspapers, Lee understood the debates between the Northern Republicans and the Democrats over the direction the war was going. Fall elections were fast approaching and he was convinced that the presence of the Army of Northern Virginia on Union soil would not look good for Lincoln. Lee's aggressive stance gained momentum with his misguided belief that the Union army lay weakened and demoralized after several mishandled confrontations.

During the dawn of September 17, a vicious attack on the Confederates by Major General Joe Hooker proved Lee wrong and set the tone for the day. Counter attacks volleyed back and forth across Miller's cornfield, in the West Woods and around Antietam Creek. Blood soaked through scores of blue and gray uniforms until the soil turned crimson.

While stationed in the woods, toward the end of the day, Alex, exhausted with cramped muscles, took his first hit. Instead of lying low during a lull in the fighting, he stood up to stretch his legs. Within seconds, a searing burn on his left forearm threw him off guard. He fell against a sturdy oak tree and slithered to the ground grasping his arm where a gaping hole in his coat sleeve oozed blood. A quick investigation revealed a second tear on the under side of his jacket. Alex breathed a sigh of relief. *The ball's gone clean through. Lucky it's a flesh wound. I can still move my arm. Gotta stop the bleeding.* He loosened the handkerchief from around his neck and looked for another soldier to help him.

Spotting a blue cap in the bushes a few feet away, he called out , "Hey, man, over here. I need help with a tourniquet." Crawling toward him, a comrade grabbed the material and tightly bound the wound.

"Thanks. I owe you."

"Nothin' owed, son. We's all in this together, but I'd make my way to the doc if I's you. No sense bleedin' to death. Getting' close to dark anyway. Time to call it a day."

Taking the soldier's advice, Alex, feeling light-headed made his way through the woods to the rear of the campsite where a temporary field hospital took in the wounded. The scene was a hive of continuous activity as wagons unloaded men of all shapes, sizes and rank. Screams of pain, cursing and moaning echoed through the still, evening air. Surgeons scurried from one man to another surveying the worst cases, often calling assistants for chloroform and a saw. The smell of putrid flesh and blood from discarded limbs piled up outside the tents and drew hordes of flies. Alex felt his stomach churn.

After waiting for what seemed to him an eternity, an assistant motioned for Alex to come forward. He took a cursory look at Alex's arm, began to untie the tourniquet, then ordered, "Gonna haf to take off your coat and shirt so's I can clean out the wound and bandage it up, soldier."

Wincing, Alex did as he was told. Standing naked to the waist, he noted scattered blood-stained rags that smelled of either carbolic acid or turpentine. The odor of both burned his nostrils and he steeled his mind and body for the cleansing liquid that doctors used to stave off putrefaction.

CONVICTIONS

Bandaged and dressed again, he made his way through the maze of men, some on cots, others lying in different positions with pained or lifeless expressions on their dirt-smudged, bearded faces. Not only did he see Union soldiers, but one section of the tent sheltered wounded, Confederate troops. Curiosity drew Alex closer. As he gazed down at them, some silent, others wrenching in agony, he noted, *take away the uniform and they're no different than us.*

As he walked on, a feeble voice caught his attention. "Water...a sip... of water, please." A bolt of fear set Alex's pulse racing. *No, it can't be. It must be someone else.*

He reached for a hanging lantern and bent over the pleading man's face. Familiar features stared back at him. *Andrew. Sue Ellen's Andrew!*

Alex grabbed the first canteen he saw, raised his brother-in-law's head and pressed the spout to his mouth. Water trickled down the man's parched lips and finally found his throat. He drank until his chest heaved with a cough and blood spat out his mouth. His eyes opened wide in recognition and he tried to speak, "A..A..."

"Yes, Andrew it's me, Alex."

Again, a tortured attempt to communicate resulted in few words. "I'm dying. Shot in...my chest."

Alex looked in vain for a surgeon but all were busy. Finding help was hopeless. He felt panic in the pit of his stomach and fought for control. *Dear God, he's my kin. What do I say to him?* Alex took Andrew's hand and held it tight. "You're not going to die alone, brother. I won't leave you."

Andrew responded with a squeeze to Alex's fingers and with a fading voice struggled to say, "Take... my ring. Bible...to Sue Ellen."

Alex waited for another word, but none came—only the last breath of a dying man. Without question, he removed the gold band on Andrew's left hand and searched the pockets of his coat for the miniature Bible. He placed his right hand on Andrew's brow, bent and kissed it before winding his way around broken bodies to escape into the evening's cool air.

The sound of shovels attacking the earth one after the other reminded Alex that Andrew would never be buried in a church cemetery, but by morning would lie in a mass grave. The thought ripped open another layer of emotion and he ran to his tent weeping.

Sitting by the fire, Willie watched as Alex ignored her presence and disappeared without a word. She waited for his return but when minutes went by, she picked up a lantern and carefully opened the tent flap. By now Alex had removed his binding coat and rolled up his left shirt sleeve, his body throbbing with sobs.

One look at this distraught man with a bandaged arm and she cried out, "You've been shot. How bad is it? She knelt beside him. "The pain must be terrible. I've never seen you so upset."

Alex wiped his eyes and ran his right sleeve across his watering nose. "The wound on my arm will heal; the wound in my heart will last forever."

Puzzled, Willie repeated, "In your heart? I don't understand."

Alex motioned for her to sit beside him and said, "My sister's husband, Andrew, was captured and brought to the field hospital. I stumbled across him by accident and he died holding my hand." Again tears rolled down his cheeks. "I pray it wasn't my bullet that struck him. He was one of the best men I've ever known. A true saint if there ever was one. He didn't deserve this. Somehow I've got to get word to Sue Ellen. But how?"

Willie put her arm around his shoulder and suggested, "Your uncle. Write to him tomorrow when you've had time to think this over and my guess is he'll find a way. He's contacted her before, remember the letter?"

Alex turned to face this woman and looked past the disguise. In his mind, he saw long golden hair flow onto fragile shoulders, crystal-clear blue eyes and a flawless complexion. *Is that true concern in her eyes? How much does she care?* He knew now what had been leading to this moment, urged on by tragedy and no guarantee for tomorrow, was a love he'd never felt before. His desire could no longer be quenched as he reached out and encircled her with his good arm then tilted her chin with his left hand. His lips sought hers, first with tenderness, then with a growing passion. The soft sigh he heard as she responded was all he needed to convince him their relationship would never be the same. Both drew back, both silent as they realized what had just transpired.

Alex spoke first. "Please don't leave. Spend the night with me. I need your company."

Willie ran her fingers across his lips and smiled. "And what kind of friend would I be if I left you here alone? Of course I'll stay."

Chapter Thirty-two

Emancipation. It was the last card General Lee expected Lincoln to pull out of his political deck. Done through Executive order, the president surmised if the slaves in the Southern states were freed, then the Confederacy would no longer be able to use them as laborers to support their field armies. Lincoln believed the stroke of the pen had the potential to weaken the enemy without countless lives taken by military force. The Union's ability at Antietam to drive Lee's forces out of Maryland gave Lincoln the initiative he needed to order a preliminary proclamation.

Reaction to this new development came from all fronts. The Abolitionists became energized, it outraged white Southerners, angered Northern Democrats and even undermined forces in Europe who considered intervening on behalf of the Confederacy. The Negroes rejoiced as the focus of the war broadened to include not only a united country, but their freedom from slavery.

Alex stoked the evening fire, his mind a thousand miles away at Oak Haven.

"You look like a man in deep thought, my friend," said Hans. "I suppose this proclamation affects your kin in a mighty big way. Don't expect your father's gonna take too fondly to it since he owns all those slaves."

"It's not my father I'm concerned about. It's Sue Ellen and Mammy. Don't know how they'll manage if all the black folk up and leave. I can only hope Joshua will stay, but who can blame him if he leaves? This proclamation coming so soon after Andrew's death has me thinking. I need to talk to Uncle Robert. I've never asked for a furlough but I'm sure I can hitch a ride into

Sharpsburg and board a train for Boston."

"What's this about Boston?" asked Willie as she emerged from her tent and joined the others.

"I need counsel from Uncle Robert and it can't wait for an exchange of letters. Since things have calmed down around here, it may be the best time to ask for a furlough." Alex saw the edges of Willie's lips droop and heard sadness in her response.

"How long will you be gone?"

"It depends on how many days Colonel Lee will give me. No more than a week, I'm sure."

Silence fell among the three of them and after several yawns, Hans got up and walked to his tent. Alex shifted his position, moved closer to Willie and in the darkness took her hand. "What's wrong? You're awfully quiet."

"Are you planning to desert? You wouldn't be the first. There's no guarantee we'll win this war—not much to come back to."

Alex squeezed Willie's hand and whispered in her ear. "There's you. And that's enough for me."

The ebbing firelight and deepening darkness provided a perfect veil as Willie removed her hand from Alex's and cupped it around the nape of his neck, pulling his head toward hers until their lips met.

After a few moments she murmured, "I'll be waiting."

***

Before boarding the train, Alex telegraphed Robert to inform him of his arrival. Once seated, he looked around at his fellow passengers. Wounded soldiers, some bandaged, others with amputated arms or legs fumbled about as they learned to cope with crutches and canes. Men in black suits and stove-top hats smoked pungent cigars while women in mourning clothes held babies and toddlers close to them.

Alex felt an air of despondency and his thoughts drifted back to the last time he traveled the rails. Excitement, eagerness, naivety and even arrogance exuded from every soldier. *How many of these men would do it all again?*

He leaned back in his seat and listened to the continuous clacking of the wheels on the tracks. It had a hypnotic effect and soon his eye lids grew heavy and he drifted off to sleep. His last thought was of Willie. He knew he couldn't stand to see the look in her eyes if he woke her to say good-bye, so he left before bugle call. Used to the booming artillery on battlefields, the sound of the hissing steam and whistle blowing did nothing to disturb Alex's much-needed rest. After several hours, the conductor nudged him and asked, "Boston your stop, son?"

Alex shook the grogginess from his head and became aware of his surrounding. "Yes, sir. Thank you. It's been quite a while since I've had this much sleep."

"And well deserved, I'm sure. You young lads are puttin' up a good fight. Me and my missus say a prayer every night that this fussin' will soon stop."

Alex shook the man's hand, picked up his haversack and departed the train to find transport to his second home.

Chapter Thirty-three

Robert McPhail stared at he stranger standing before him. *Could this be Alex?* Where was the robust, ruddy-complexioned nephew he sent off to war? Instead, he saw a gaunt, pale-faced male with a diminished frame and weary, sad eyes. But one feature had not changed—the warmth of his smile. Both men embraced as Alex stepped into the atrium of his uncle's home.

"Welcome, Alex. It's so good to see you. There hasn't been a day since you left when this family hasn't brought you to mind." Robert turned toward the parlor and called, "He's here, girls. Your cousin is back."

Within seconds, Alex heard squeals of laughter and the swish of taffeta skirts as Coreen and Jenny raced down the hallway to smoother Alex in hugs and kisses. Aunt Abigail and Bessie followed. Even Henry appeared and shook his hand.

Robert gave a hearty laugh. "Enjoy the attention, son. For the next few days try to put the war behind you. Now let's eat. Bessie's prepared a meal that's bound to put some meat back on your bones."

Seated around the table, everyone held hands as Robert gave a blessing. At the last 'amen', Alex continued to bow his head and added, "Thank you, Lord, for this loving family, the protection you've given me and comrades who'll live in my heart forever."

The smells and sights of food he'd not tasted for almost two years overwhelmed him and out of habit took a small portion of roast beef, mashed potatoes, gravy, peas, corn and freshly baked bread. Abigail noticed her nephew's hesitancy and encouraged him to fill his plate.

"There's more in the kitchen, Alex, help yourself. Bessie will be pleased if you go for seconds."

Alex felt a flush of embarrassment and quickly explained, "Oh, it's not that I don't care for her delicious food. I haven't had a decent meal in months." He hesitated then added, "It's just that I feel guilty knowing my friends are eating fried pork and hardtack day after day."

Coreen was first to comment. "Surely they wouldn't begrudge you a chance to eat properly. Besides, we plan to send you back with smoked meats, dried fruit and all sorts of goodies from the pantry you can share with them."

"I assure you they'll appreciate your generosity." Alex smiled at his cousin. "Okay, I wouldn't want to upset Bessie, so please pass me the roast beef again."

***

Alex relaxed in warm, soothing bath water while Henry cut his hair and shaved two day's growth from his whiskered face. These simple acts restored Alex's spirit and gave him time to talk to his new friend.

"I haven't told Uncle Robert yet, but Sue Ellen's husband, Andrew, is dead. Shot in the chest."

Henry gasped. "No, your sister don' deserve dat. She one kind lady. Treat me like family when I was dere. Your father..." Henry shook his head. "Dat's a different story."

"No need to explain. He'll never change. I'm sure emancipation has embittered him even more. But let me tell you how I found Andrew. He was still alive and wanted me to take his wedding ring and Bible to send back to Sue Ellen. I sat with him until he died. It was true co-incidence."

A sliver of a smile creased the edges of Henry's lips. "Ain't no co-incidence, Alex. The Almighty brought you two together. He don' want Andrew to die alone."

Alex pondered this humble man's words before commenting, "I hope you're right. You've given me something to think about."

Chapter Thirty-four

Alex indulged in the luxury of sleeping in a regular bed and didn't awaken until the sun sent streams of light dancing across his feather pillow. He sat up with a start, threw back the covers and jumped to the floor expecting to hear roll call. Unfamiliar surroundings brought him back to reality. He looked around for his uniform but instead found a clean shirt, britches, jacket and shoes laid out for him. He dressed with haste and found his way to the kitchen.

Bessie, with hands covered in flour, saw him first. "Good mornin'. I hope you slept well."

"Yes, ma'am. We don't get much sleep in the Infantry. Up with the sunrise every day."

"Well, I knows you hungry, so sit yo'self down and I git you a Yankee breakfast. Henry, pour the lad some coffee."

Henry followed his wife's order and gave Alex a pat on the shoulder as he placed the steaming black liquid before him. "See baby, our lad's lookin' better already and he ain't here a full day yet."

"I feel a lot better, too." Alex took a sip of coffee and asked, "Where is everyone?"

"The ladies gone shoppin' and Mr. Robert at his office. He want me to bring you down there when you's ready. He anxious to hear all 'bout the war from your side. He say it better to talk privately since there may be things you rather the women don't need to hear. Besides, they buzz around you like bees to honey." Henry chuckled, "I thinks they sweet on you, Alex."

"I have to admit, they've always treated me well. I consider myself lucky to have them as cousins."

Henry bent over Bessie's shoulder, placed a kiss on the nape of her neck and said, "A man needs a good woman. When you git home from war, I hopes you find yours."

Alex smiled as Willie's face came to mind and he mused, *I've found mine, Henry. If I can keep the Rebs from killing her there'll be no need to look any further.*

The smell of fried potatoes, onions, ham and eggs displaced any further thoughts of war and he dug in to clean his plate.

***

"I've tried to imagine a soldier's life these days and it stymies my imagination, Alex. Let me hear it from someone who's fresh from the field. Is it as horrible as I hear?" Robert leaned across his desk and gave his nephew his full attention.

"It's hell, sir. There's no way you can imagine unless you've experienced hunger, thirst, panic, unfavorable weather and fear rolled into one huge nightmare with no end in sight. From the beginning, confusion and misguided leadership has plagued the Union Army. We seem to be climbing a slippery pole—win a battle, lose a battle. Never seem to be able to stay on top."

Robert interjected, "Our sources tell us that Lincoln has had enough of this timidity and 'wait and see' attitude General McClellan demonstrates. Don't be surprised if a change of leadership happens before Christmas. Emancipation has invigorated we abolitionists like never before, so Henry and I are planning a trip down south to spread the word among the plantations slaves that their day has come."

Alex looked at his uncle with surprise. "You're going to Oak Haven?"

Henry answered. "We hopin' to see your friend, Joshua. He smart and I figures he help his folk understand they no longer beholden to your father."

"And of course, Sue Ellen," broke in Robert. A frown deepened the lines on his forehead and he took a deep breath before

CONVICTIONS

saying, "Even my brother if he'll see me."

At this point, Alex announced with a catch in his throat, "Andrew's dead. Sue Ellen's husband was shot in the chest at Antietam." His eyes watered and he wiped a tear away. "I thought it best to tell you alone."

Robert gasped and dropped his head in his hands. A moment of silence followed before he spoke. "How terrible! There soon won't be a family in this nation not touched by the atrocities of this war. But are you sure?"

Alex repeated the events as he told them to Henry.

"I do have a favor to ask now that you're going south."

"A letter?" asked Robert.

"More than a letter. Andrew's last wish was that Sue Ellen get his wedding ring and Bible. They're in my haversack at the house. It would mean so much to her."

"Of course, son, I'd feel honored."

"I have to warn you she may not even know he's dead. Sometimes it takes months for families to get the news they've lost a loved one."

"No need to worry; I'll handle the situation. Returning Andrew's belongings should help ease the pain." A gentleness erased the concern on Robert's face and he reached into his jacket pocket and handed Alex an envelope. "I want you to take this money and use it however you wish. Go about town and give yourself time to relax. Enjoy this furlough."

Alex protested, "Uncle, I've saved my monthly pay and my needs are small. You've been more than kind."

"Listen, I know the pittance the government gives you lads. It's shameful, especially when you risk your lives every day. No, it's the least I can do." Robert paused then asked, "Alex, just a couple more questions."

"Certainly, sir."

"Is your heart convinced you made the right choice? Is the Union still worth saving after all the carnage this war has caused?"

Alex straightened his shoulders and said, "My convictions

haven't changed, but my perspective on war has caused me to wonder if there couldn't have been a better alternative to solve the problems." The tone in his voice saddened, "But it's too late now, isn't it?"

***

With the extra money, Alex bought a new uniform to replace his bullet-torn, tattered one. He wore it with pride striding down the streets of Boston and often citizens, young and old, patted him on the arm and repeated the same refrain, "Good work soldier. Please don't give up."

A photographer's shingle caught Alex's eye and he seized the moment. *Why not send a recent photo to Sue Ellen by way of Uncle Robert? There's so little I can do to lessen the pain she'll soon bear. Maybe seeing my image will help."*

Browsing among the display of photos, Alex saw the perfect gift for Willie. An open locket held a miniature picture of a Union soldier holding a rifle. *She can wear it under her shirt close to her heart and no one will know.*

"Come back tomorrow," the photographer said as Alex prepared to leave, "They'll be waiting for you. Much as I hate to admit it, this war has been great for business." He patted Alex on the shoulder and offered his advice. "Keep your head low and your aim straight."

Chapter Thirty-five

After five days, as much as Alex hated to leave the generous hospitality, laughter and security of his relatives, he felt a longing to once again join his company—especially, Willie. *Did she miss me?*

His question dissipated the moment he saw her carrying a bucket of water to the tents. She dropped the pail, spilling its content, and came running to his side smiling and babbling. "You did come back! Hans, Alex is back. And look at you, all shaved and wearing a new uniform." Willie looked around her and seeing no one looking in her direction, tugged at Alex's arm until they were hidden inside her tent. With no hesitation, she wrapped her arms around his neck and kissed him before he could say a word.

He responded in kind then broke their embrace with these words, "Close your eyes and hold out your hand. No peeking."

Her child-like giggle ended with, "A surprise for me?"

Alex pulled the locket from his breast pocket, placed it in her trembling hand and instructed, "Now you can open them."

Willie's breath caught in her throat as the shiny metal, in the shape of a heart, glistened before her. Tears spilled over her rosy cheeks and for a moment she was speechless.

Seeing her emotion, Alex said, "There's more; let me open it for you."

She wiped her eyes dry and stared at the photo inside. "It's you. My own forever."

"Wear it under your shirt and I'll know it's close to your heart." Alex clasped the chain around her neck and kissed the tip of an ear.

By now, Hans entered and held out his arms to embrace his friend. "We've missed you. Not much has happened since you left, but come and eat. I've snared a rabbit and it's roasting as we talk."

"And with it we'll have dried fruit and fresh bread—compliments of my family."

"Bless them," echoed brother and sister.

Chapter Thirty-six

"No, this is wrong. Why are we battling in the heart of Fredericksburg? We're not trained to fight in the streets." Willie's eyes darted from one shattered building to another trying to detect Rebel snipers in cellars, attics and fences.

"Because it's war and General Burnside's strategy is to take the city before Lee's men get a foothold, replied Hans."

"We're too late," said Alex. "Our pontoon boats and the material to build bridges over the Rappahannock should have been here two weeks ago. Bureaucracy stinks. We carry the brunt of decision makers in Washington and now the Rebs have the advantage. Look at how many of our men were killed this morning trying to get us across this river."

"So that's why when we woke this morning the order was given to shell and dismantle every house, shop, church and anything else standing," raged Willie. "I'm not proud to be forcing unarmed, innocent civilians from their homes." She suddenly left formation, scooped up a frightened youngster in her arms and returned him to a frantic mother.

"Forgive us ma'am; here's your lost child. Hang onto him. It's going to get worse."

House fires, and artillery smoke invaded the town causing mass confusion and companies scattered in all directions. Men on a frenzy entered homes and businesses carrying out confiscated bounty.

"Shame, shame on our troops," scolded Willie. "Where are the officers to demand order?"

"All we can do is stick together and defend ourselves," offered

Hans. "Trouble is, we can't see what's waiting for us around these dang corners."

Urban fighting continued until dusk and the order from the top was that all Union troops stationed in Fredericksburg would find shelter anywhere it was available. No camping fires allowed.

Huddled together for warmth in the cellar of a shelled apothecary, Hans, Willie and Alex nibbled on rations of dry bread and figs as each took turns dozing. An occasional whistle of Minie´ balls striking the building kept everyone's nerves on edge. By dawn, commanding officers rode up and down the streets calling their companies into formation.

As the fog lifted, the Twentieth Massachusetts searched for their dead and a mass burial performed. A dwindling number of troops followed Colonel Hall through the ravaged streets out to Telegraph Road where unseen behind a stone wall waited the enemy. Up above, on Marye's Hill, General Lee, with his artillery ready to strike, watched as Confederate rifles opened fire and Union men of all ages, size and rank fell.

Hans, felt the sting of a bullet graze his scalp, knocking his cap to the ground as he swirled about dazed. A flow of blood trickled down his face and Willie looked up to see her brother hit the dusty, well-trodden earth. Her scream caught Alex's attention and he rushed to her side.

"Hans, talk to me." Willie cried, " Open your eyes."

Alex found the source of blood and assured her the wound was superficial. "It's only a graze. He's lucky."

By now, Hans regained his senses and squirmed to get up. "My cap—I need my cap."

Willie spotted it a few feet away and quickly retrieved the bullet-torn covering and placed it over the clotting wound.

The order to fall back came as a fresh company arrived to relieve the Twentieth. Several attempts by the grand division of the Army of the Potomac to dislodge the Confederates from the heights were repulsed until victory was hopeless.

Refusing to accept the fact that his battle plans went awry, Burnside insisted on his officers leading demoralized troops into

CONVICTIONS

battle the following day. Mortality rates soared and blue uniforms covered the field as far as the eye could see. Retreat across the river meant defeat, to continue meant total massacre.

Chapter Thirty-seven

The sound of saws gnawing at pine trees and the rat-tat-tat of hammers assembling wooden huts at Falmouth outdid the curious screeching jay birds. The Twentieth Massachusetts settled in for the winter on the opposite side of the Rappahannock not far from the Rebels in Fredericksburg.

Up to now, winter campaigns brought a break from constant marching and battle strategy. That is until General Burnside, humiliated by the Union's defeat in December, decided to devise his own plan.

"Burnside's up to something," said Hans as he warmed his hands over flames in the make-shift fireplace. He keeps riding up and down the river bank looking across at the Rebs."

"My guess is he figures his time is short as commander if he doesn't do something to restore his reputation." added Alex. "Lincoln's sacked better men than him."

Willie looked upward and cried out, "Dear God, please don't send us across the river again."

But that was Burnside's plan. He ordered pontoon boats be carried to a narrower crossing at Bank's Ford. His intention was to send troops across to surprise Lee's left flank, thus drawing them into the open.

No one anticipated a turn of events, but the night of January 20, Mother Nature sent a warning.

"Winds pickin' up, guys," a picket announced as he came off duty and joined a group around a fire. A light rain comin' in fast over yonder."

"Doesn't sound good for tomorrow's plan," a seasoned soldier spoke his mind. "I hate's marchin' in the rain. Feet get wet and cold. Tires you plumb out. If I ever get home, I swear I'll never walk in the rain no more."

Not only did the rain begin in earnest over the night but the winds howled as a nor'easter let loose it's fury. By morning, the dirt roads were transformed into a muddy quagmire. Still, Burnside ordered the pontoons, artillery and men to forge ahead. Loaded wagons sank in the mud as horses floundered to keep moving a few feet at a time. Taxed to their limit, they fell dead from exhaustion.

To make matters worse, Lee figured out Burnside's plan and used this time to fortify his left flank. Close to the crossing, Rebel voices taunted the men with shouts of "This way to Richmond. Come on over."

After much cussing and grumbling among the men, Burnside, desperate to keep the troops spirits alive, distributed rations of whiskey, but this effort turned against him and before long a drunken melee broke out.

After a flying fist barely missed Willie's brow, Hans grabbed his sister under her arms and lifted her to safety. "Damned foolishness. As if things aren't bad enough, the man gives out alcohol. What was he thinking? He's got to go. McClellan would never have done such a thing."

A chorus of cheers from those nearby agreed with Hans and they lifted him high in the air, his feet dangling—naked.

"Where are your shoes?" asked Willie. Her voice held authority. "Put him down."

Within seconds, his feet were covered in mire. "Stuck in the mud about a mile back. It was either leave them or get trampled. I ain't the only one. Others got the same problem. Better than a bullet stuck in me. Besides, I hear that there's extra shoes at the field hospital. Surgeons take 'em off the amputated legs."

"I'd make that your first stop if we ever get back to camp," suggested Alex. "Sounds like there may be a line."

***

CONVICTIONS

Broken by exhaustion, death and stubborn Burnside strategy, the army's morale plummeted and many deserted. Finally after four days, he ordered the men back to Falmouth. Burnside resigned the next day and Lincoln wasted no time in replacing him with Maj. General Joseph Hooker.

Chapter Thirty-eight

Spring brought relief from the winter doldrums and with a change of command came a return to orderliness reminiscent of Colonel Lee's and McClellan's days. Hooker dispersed discontented feelings with extensive grantings of furloughs, fresh weekly rations of bread, potatoes, onions, and dried vegetables so necessary to ward off scurvy.

Since it had been four months since Alex had talked to Robert, he became anxious to know if the trip his uncle and Henry planned to Oak Haven had been successful. He knew such a mission to proclaim the meaning of the Emancipation act to the Negroes involved time and considerable risk. The apprehension that surfaced in his mind daily was put to rest when he received a packet of letters the first of April.

With trembling fingers, Alex tore open the envelope and began to read:

Dear Alex:

Only by the grace of God, did Henry and I return to Boston in one piece. Although the news we brought to the Negroes was well received, to others, owners and white elitists, they would rather keep their slaves in bondage. Our lives were threatened on more than one occasion. But the truth can not be hidden and we have already seen the fruits of our labor as hundreds have left the plantations and headed north. Even as I write this letter, a black regiment is being trained to enter the Army of the Potomac.

Now, let me bring matters of a more personal nature to your attention. When we arrived at Oak Haven, we saw a wreath of mourning on the front door. I immediately assumed Sue Ellen had word of Andrew's death, but I was mistaken. For an instant, Alex lifted his eyes from the paper and his mind questioned. *Who could it be? Mammy? Joshua? Father?*

Searching for the answer, he continued to read. *Your father is dead. He died in February of heart failure. I regret I arrived too late for any chance of reconciliation. I'll let Sue Ellen's letter provide more detail.*

Sue Ellen had no idea Andrew was killed at Antietam and I have to admit it was difficult adding to her grief. She was more than grateful to receive her husband's possessions. The ring now hangs on a chain around her neck and every day she reads from Andrew's Bible.

From what I've read in the papers, these past few months have been rough for our troops, but the battle is not over until it is over, so keep strong and my sincerest sympathy to you on the loss of your father. Try to forgive; we are commanded by a Higher authority to do so or it will destroy us.

God Bless,
Robert

Stunned by the news of his father's death, anger suddenly surged through Alex's body and he beat the sleeping mat with his fist until his arm ached. Guilt mixed with pride and sorrow brought tears and his body shook until he felt spent of emotion.

Gaining control, Alex reached for the second letter in the packet. His heart ached for Sue Ellen. *How is she coping with two recent deaths?*

The envelope smelled of lavender, his sister's favorite fragrance, and he reminded himself to pass it on to Willie who loved it too. As Alex unfolded the sheets of stationary, he noticed stains that ran into the ink. *Can these be her tears?*

Dearest Alex,

By now you probably have heard from Uncle Robert that Father died in February and is now lying beside Mother at the church cemetery. For the past year, his health had not been good. It was an effort for him to walk any distance without com-

plaining of fatigue and pain in his chest. The doctor diagnosed a failing heart. When Emancipation became law, I saw a quick decline and he refused to get out of bed.

I understand if you cannot find it in your heart to shed any tears over him, but deep down I know he loved you. It was his stubborn pride that inhibited him from showing forgiveness.

This is the hardest part of this letter to write, but I'm full of gratitude you were with Andrew when he died. The Confederate Army may post the deaths of our troops at a public building but no effort is made to contact the families. I can't thank our uncle enough for the trip he made to return Andrew's belongings.

I still look for my husband's letters and then I realize there'll be no more words from him. Memories are all I've got, but I'm so thankful our marriage was based on God's love for us. Everlasting. Some day you'll find your mate, Alex. She'll be a lucky woman because I know you well.

We all long to see you soon. Much love.

Sue Ellen

Later that evening, Alex asked Willie to join him for a walk in the woods. He handed her the letters and asked her to read them. He wanted to see how she would react to his invitation to share a raw, personal part of his life with her. Alex got the reaction he hoped for when she looked at him with empathy and tears in her eyes. When finished, she reached for him and together they held each other in silence. *No words are necessary; she understands my grief.* The sound of taps reminded them their time together was brief. But the taste of her lips gave him comfort from the day's news and it was well after dark when they snuck back into camp.

Chapter Thirty-nine

Pressure from Lincoln to capture Richmond meant Hooker needed to break through Lee's forces around Fredericksburg, capture Chancellorsville and move on to the Confederate capital. His strategy looked good on paper but as the troops discovered it was not well executed.

Hooker sent three corps to circumvent Lee's smaller numbers in hopes of drawing Confederate troops out of the woods and into the open. Lee out-witted him and refused to leave the tangled, thickets. Heavy fighting ensued with mounting casualties on both sides. When Stonewall Jackson's men used the cover of night to place themselves behind Hooker's rear flank, the next day Hooker lost his nerve and abandoned key ground. Once again the Union Army retreated across the river.

Anger and criticism from officers who were ready to fight exclaimed, "Thought he was known as "Fighting Joe Hooker". Sure didn't live up to his reputation. Wait 'til Lincoln hears about this. We'll be getting us a new commander."

***

By June the soldiers were restless. "We can't leave this forsaken soil fast enough," complained a soldier poking a stick into the campfire. "Defeat and bloodshed's all we've seen since we've been here."

Another man added, "Looks like this will be our last night looking across the river since Lee's left Fredericksburg and headed north. Spies tell us the Rebs need food and supplies. The

Shenandoah Valley's a likely spot to replenish. Lots of fertile farms and Jackson took it back not long ago. Course he's dead now—shot by one of his own on picket duty. Big loss for the Rebs."

"It's gonna be a long haul, fellas. Lincoln's countin' on the Army of the Potomac to keep Lee out of Washington. This past year's been pretty good for the Rebs and it looks like Lee's got his eye on a final victory on our territory."

"Not if my ole legs are still standin' and I can fire a rifle," stated a veteran trooper. A chorus of agreement settled the matter and men dispersed to their quarters.

***

Days of marching over hills, through woods and across rivers pursuing the Confederate Army finally came to a climax in Gettysburg, Pennsylvania. Tension built as reports trickled down through the Union ranks that skirmishes inside the town had driven the Yankees out to Cemetery Ridge. Not only was there uncertainty concerning the Union strategy, but three days before their arrival, Lincoln replaced Hooker with General George Mead who had little time to plan and get to know his men.

The Twentieth Massachusetts arrived late the night of July 2 and joined a 'fish hook' defensive position along a ridge with the other regiments. Cannon and artillery smoke from the day's battles settled over the area and an eerie foreboding urged Alex to speak to Willie before she fell asleep.

"Willie, we need to talk. Sit up and look at me."

"Now? I'm too tired." She pulled her covering over her shoulders. "Can't it wait 't'il daybreak? My legs are killing me."

Alex placed his hands on her shoulders and forced her to a sitting position.

"Listen to me. The word among the troops is that Lee's prepared to come at us with full force tomorrow and I've made a decision."

"No, Alex, you can't desert. It's too late now and it's dangerous. Please don't go." She threw her arms around his neck and pulled him close.

"I'm not going anywhere but I hope you do. When I discovered your identity I told you if things got worse I would turn you in. I believe we've reached that stage."

Alex felt Willie's body tremble and he heard fear as she pleaded, "No, Alex, please don't send me away." Her fear turned to anger. "How can you tell me you love me then deceive me like this?"

By now the tears that saturated her cheeks threatened to weaken Alex's resolve. "It's because I love you that you can't stay. I've already discussed this with Hans and he agrees with me."

Willie pulled back and buried her face in her arms. The hurt in her words hit their mark. "No. Not Hans, too? You've turned my brother against me. I have no place to go."

Alex lifted her chin and his voice softened. "Yes, you have. I've written to Uncle Robert explaining our situation. I know he'll take you into their home. My cousins are your age and would be happy to welcome you. When the war is over, I'll come for you and we can make our future plans."

Again anger stiffened her limbs and she pulled further away.

"You've already contacted your uncle?"

"No. The letter is written but I've not yet sent it. If we live through tomorrow, the choice is yours." Alex stopped and let his words penetrate. "Either I send the letter and you'll have a decent home, or I talk to the Colonel and God only knows where they'll send you."

Alex stood, his face solemn and stated one more time. "The choice is yours, Willie. Goodnight."

Chapter Forty

July 4, 1863

The chirping of robins woke Alex as they hopped about in the trampled grass scavenging for worms. Between the week's long march and yesterday's fierce fighting, his exhausted mind was in a fog. He rolled off his mat and opened the tent flap expecting to see Willie making coffee as she always did. But there was no sign of her. *Maybe she's still sleeping. Can't blame her.* Alex walked to her tent and peeked in. Empty. *Hmmm, maybe she's looking for water.*

He looked out over the landscape strewn with bodies. His nostrils filled with the smell of death. Within seconds, the fog in his brain dissipated and clarity ushered in the bitter truth. Willie wasn't coming back. Scenes of yesterday's battle flashed before his eyes as he recalled each horrible moment. He had instructed her to stay close to him. Then out of the corner of his eye he saw the cannon belch its fiery wrath in their direction, and he yelled, "stay low!" Too late. Flying shrapnel found its target. *The sound of her screams will haunt me forever.* With an aching heart and riddled with guilt, Alex doubled over and fell to the earth weeping as low, guttural moans caught in his throat.

***

A victory for the Army of the Potomac held little joy for Hans and Alex.

"I'm going into Gettysburg to find my sister, Alex. Come with me. There's sure to be talk about a disguised woman losing a leg fighting for the Union. Someone has to know where they took her."

"I'm with you, but we'll have to talk to the General or they'll brand us deserters."

A stern-faced sergeant stationed outside General Meade's tent refused the men entry. "Don't you know he's busy planning our next move. Last night Lee packed up and left. Probably heading south to Virginia. We need to stop him. Lincoln's counting on it so there's no time to lose. Whatever your complaint is it'll have to wait."

A commanding voice from within the tent ordered. "Hush, Sergeant. Send the boys in."

After the regulatory salute and introduction, General Meade listened as Alex and Hans pled their case. When finished, a few moments of silence passed before their commander spoke. "You mean to tell me a woman has fought with the Twentieth Massachusetts for two years and no superior officers knew it?" A twinkle in the General's eye eased the tension. "Now that's a lady I'd like to meet."

"Yes, sir." said Hans. "My sister is quite a woman—one of a kind, isn't she Alex?"

Alex felt a flush of red creep up his neck before he answered. "Oh, that she is, sir. That she is."

General Meade cleared his throat and resumed his commanding composure. "Of course you two knew the army takes a dim view of such things and yet you played along with her. Surely it must have crossed your minds something like this would happen to a woman."

"Sir," Alex defended their position. "We begged her to leave on several occasions, but her convictions for a united county run deep. Besides, Hans is the only family she has. Willie refused to leave him."

General Meade leaned back in his chair and studied the young soldiers. His expression became serious and he said, "How do I know this isn't a ploy to desert your company? Leave with my permission then head off to parts unknown."

Alex made eye contact with his commander and never flinched as he answered, "All we can offer is our word, sir. And two years of loyal service to the Union Army."

A moment of silence followed and General Meade's demeanor shifted from a formal stance to one of compassion. "I'll give you five hours. Report back to me on your return. Hitch a ride into Gettysburg on one of the supply wagons and check every public building. With the number of casualties yesterday, every available space is being used."

"Thank you, sir." Alex and Hans spoke in unison. As they turned to leave, General Meade had the last word. "Private, Baden."

Hans straightened his shoulders and gave him his attention. "Yes, sir."

"You're a hardened soldier who's seen death all around you." He paused. "But this is your sister and she may not have made it. I pray I'm wrong. You're dismissed."

***

The town of Gettysburg bore the brunt of battle. Shattered glass from store shops littered the streets and overturned wagons and crates were riddled with bullet holes. Even the buildings had chunks of brick torn away leaving holes and scars. Charred timbers that once supported wooden structures continued to burn and smoke rose in spirals.

The main street over-flowed with a mixture of celebration and despair. On the town square an army band played patriotic tunes while ambulance wagons continued to haul in those that were lucky enough to have survived the night on the field.

"Where should we start, Alex? Why are all these people milling about?"

"Curiosity seekers. I suggest we follow that ambulance. Looks to me like that church up ahead may be turned into a hospital."

Pushing their way through the crowd, Alex and Hans rushed

up the steps to the First Baptist Church of Gettysburg to find row after row of wounded soldiers. Male and female nurses went from one to the other giving water, food or simply a kind word of comfort. The smell of chloroform, blood, rotting flesh and vomit threatened to send them back out into the morning air, but they were on a mission.

Hans stopped an attendant and asked, "My sister may be here and I'm desperate to find her. She lost her leg yesterday in battle and they took her away."

The woman looked at Hans with disbelief and said, "A woman? This church is full of wounded soldiers—men who fought valiantly and may still lose their lives. I've been here for two days and no woman has appeared. Believe me."

"May we look for ourselves, ma'am?" asked Alex, "He's telling the truth. She fought in disguise."

"Go ahead. You know she may be somewhere else. The court house is now a hospital, too. And some of the larger homes in town." She placed a hand on Han's arm and her voice softened, "I hope you find her."

***

The sun climbed higher in the sky and the hours slipped by, but even though Alex and Hans scoured every possible makeshift hospital, Willie was nowhere to be seen.

"How could she just disappear? It makes no sense. Every other wounded soldier is somewhere in this town. Now we've run out of time."

Alex stopped his friend and as they stood face to face, his eyes watered and his voice trembled, "We both have high hopes of finding Willie, but just as General Meade made it clear, some don't make it. Maybe that's why we can't find her."

"No," Hans's voice amplified and caught the attention of those around them. "She's not dead. How can you say such a thing? You loved her."

"I will always love your sister. Make no mistake, I'll do everything in my power to find her—dead or alive." Alex put his arm around Hans's drooping shoulder. "C'mon, General Meade is expecting us."

Chapter Forty-One

"I tell you, Colonel, we'll not leave until every dead soldier out there, Union or Confederate, is buried."

"But sir, President Lincoln expects the Army of the Potomac to capture what's left of Lee's army before they cross into Virginia. This is our chance to end this terrible conflict. With every day we tarry, our enemy slips away."

"Must I remind you who is in command?" General Meade's sharpened tone put an end to the conversation. "Now get out there and have your men start digging the graves. Mass burials are the least we can do for these brave men—and that includes Lee's Rebels. And it wouldn't hurt if you picked up a shovel yourself."

For the next few days, the sound of wagons transporting the dead to huge holes in the earth before vultures picked at any remaining flesh on their bones became a familiar sight. Finally, the order to break camp and move south toward the Potomac River came as a relief.

With every step Alex took away from Gettysburg, the hole in his heart grew deeper. *Where is my little soldier who marched beside me in perfect formation?* Every now and again, his head turned to the left, as it had numerous times in the past, to see if Willie was keeping pace. Each time this happened, he swung back to the front with tears in his eyes.

For three days, the swollen waters of the Potomac River prevented Lee's Army from crossing into the safety of Virginia. But even with this delay in their retreat, the Union troops let an opportunity to engage in a final battle for total victory slip by.

Meade's men reached the river a day too late. The Army of Northern Virginia was gone. Lincoln was furious. He expected a hot pursuit after victory at Gettysburg, but instead Meade reported he was satisfied to have driven the enemy out of northern territory. Disappointed once again in generals who did not appear to have the will to finish the task, the President turned his eyes west to a man who demonstrated intelligence, military experience and the will to end the war no matter what it took.

Ulysses S. Grant rose in the ranks to command the capture of Fort Henry and Fort Donelson on the Tennessee River, followed by the fall of Vicksburg on the Mississippi. Lincoln was convinced Grant was the man needed to take offensive action against the south and he commissioned him to the position of General-in-chief, March 10, 1864.

The newspapers were abuzz with commentaries and predictions concerning Lincoln's choice of General-in-chief after so many battle disappointments. The morale of the troops in the field soared.

"We finally got us a man with some guts," was a common opinion. "Let's get on with this business of war, we want to go home."

***

"Mail call," the courier's announcement never failed to catch the men's attention. The earth shook with the stampede of feet rushing to receive news from the 'home front'.

Alex and Hans waited until the last soldier's name was called, but their anticipation turned to disappointment time and time again. No letter from Willie.

"You're torturing yourselves, fellas," suggested the courier. He turned the canvas bag upside down and shook it hard. "Nope. Ain't no letter stuck in the bottom. Might as well face the truth—there may never be."

"I know, I know," confessed Hans, "but as close as my sister and I were it's hard to believe she wouldn't write. She must be dead."

Alex spoke up. "A sensible man would accept that conclusion, but I haven't given up yet. Listen, Hans, yesterday I met a fella from Pennsylvania and we got talking about Gettysburg and how we wished Grant had been in command then. Both of us agreed the war would have likely been over. He never would have let Lee cross the Potomac."

"So what's that got to do with Willie?"

"It happens that his sister lives in Gettysburg. Don't you get it? She could have heard about Willie and what happened to her. Folks in small towns know everything that goes on."

"Okay, so what can we do? Almost a year has passed and we're miles away headin' for Richmond again. Grant's determined this time we'll take it."

"We can't do much of anything, but this guy, Nathan, offered to write his sister and ask her to start asking questions around town. It's worth a try; I lay awake at night living this nightmare over and over in my mind."

Hans nodded. "You're not the only one. But what if nothing comes of it?"

"Then we try again; I refuse to give up hope. I know she'd do the same if it were one of us."

Chapter Forty-Two

May, 1864, Sisters of Mercy Convent

"Sister Mary, come quickly." A young nun ran into the kitchen of the convent and tugged at the elder nun's tunic.

"Merciful Lord, what is it child?"

"Winona. She's in the chapel on her knees sobbing. I tried to comfort her but she ignored me as though I wasn't there. Something has greatly disturbed her."

"Many people have cried in humility before the Lord my dear. Perhaps she was in deep prayer."

"But she's holding a locket in her hand—not a rosary."

Sister Mary stopped stirring a bowl of flour and sugar. A look of bewilderment knit her brows together. "I'll handle this, Sister. You go along and finish your work."

Beneath the statue of Christ, illuminated by burning candles, was a young woman, drenched in tears, clinging to a metal locket.

"Winona, my child," whispered Sister Mary as she bent down and placed an arm around her shoulders, "what's troubling you?"

Overwrought with emotion, Winona buried her head in the Sister's bosom and through sentence fragments cried, " I remember—it's all coming back to me."

"What do you remember?"

"The war. I was a soldier. The noise—guns and cannons. Men running everywhere. Confusion. It was horrible." Another round of sobs ensued.

"Who was with you dear? Were you alone?"

Winona wiped her eyes with the sleeve of her dress. She pondered a moment before she raised her head. "No, I was with my brother—Hans. And Alex." She raised the opened locket and stared at the photo inside. "We were in love."

Sister Mary, unnerved by this unbelievable tale, rose, handed Winona her crutch and said, "Come sit with me. Try to recall what happened before you came to us. It's been almost a year ago."

Hobbling across to a bench, a sudden revelation struck Winona and she looked down her left side where the lower part of her leg was missing. A gasp crossed her lips as the moment of terror came back to her. She stumbled and almost fell before Sister Mary reached out and caught her.

"Take your time. Breathe deeply."

A few seconds passed before Winona's mind unlocked the events of her past.

"We were ready for battle. Alex lay on the ground beside me. I heard the cannon blast. Then pain shot through my leg." She closed her eyes and the muscles in her face contracted. "Unbearable pain. And that's all I remember until I opened my eyes and saw you."

For the next hour, the two women talked while Winona's memory opened up and her words flowed in an ever-ending stream. Sister Mary learned about her family history and time spent at the orphanage, her plot to disguise herself as a male to keep close to Hans and her relationship with Alex—her first love.

Sister Mary took Winona's hand and asked, "Do you want to try and contact your brother? Someone in the war department in Washington must know where the Twentieth Massachusetts is located. After all this time with no word from you, he may think you died."

"Maybe it's better that way." Winona's voice grew somber. "Besides, he may be gone, too. Union soldiers die every time they fight the Rebels. I couldn't stand it if that's what's happened to him. So it's best not knowing." A lone tear trickled down her cheek.

"Winona, I don't believe you really feel that way. You've had a terrible shock to your body and you may not be thinking clearly.

Is there something else that's bothering you? Something you're holding back that you're afraid to tell me?"

Winona hung her head in silence and pursed her lips in a thin line. Sister Mary saw that it was futile to pressure her into some confession, so she stood and in a motherly fashion said, "I'll leave you alone, dear. Remember, there is one who is always willing to listen. Talk to Him. He'll give you peace."

The door to the chapel almost closed when Winona called out, "Sister, forgive me. Yes, I am afraid. If I tell Hans, Alex is sure to find out and he'll want no more of me. What man wants a woman with half a leg missing? I can't face the humiliation or the pity."

"Think on it, Winona. It's one way to know if this young man's love for you is true."

Sister Mary turned to look at the statue of Christ, made the sign of the cross and walked away.

Chapter Forty-three

The long awaited letter from Nathan's sister arrived in May as the Twentieth Massachusetts trudged south-east through dense, humid wilderness, deep ravines and open spaces. Weary to the bone, Hans and Alex felt rejuvenated by the news the letter contained.

"Here fellas," Nathan handed a soiled, wrinkled envelope to Alex, "finally word from my sister that may be what you're lookin' for. Read it yourselves."

Both men regained a surge of energy as Alex began:
Brother Nathan,

How interesting that you should relate the story of a disguised women in your regiment who was injured. In fact, for several months after the siege of Gettysburg, rumors were heard around town that such a woman existed. However, they could never be proven as it seems she disappeared.

I reopened the discussion at a women's sewing circle and a cousin of ours told me that her husband delivers milk to a convent outside of town and often sees a young women on crutches working in the kitchen. He swears she was not there before the battles. The nuns have been known to take in refugees but are very closed-mouth about them. This may or may not be the lady in question, but it's the best I can do to help.

Alex stopped reading at this point and a smile lit up his beaded, sun-baked face.

"Hans, a fifty-fifty chance it may be Willie is better than none at all."

"You're right." He looked at Nathan and shook his hand.

"Thank you, friend. You've given me back some hope of finding my sister."

Chapter Forty-four

Over the next six weeks, brutal battles at the Wilderness, Spotsylvania and Cold Harbor left behind multitudes of Union soldiers dead, some of which were the result of Grant's errors. No longer was the Napoleonic method of two forces lining up against each other working. The improved accuracy and power of the rifled muskets and the Minie´ ball mowed down targeted men line after line. As the war continued, both Lee and Grant realized that a shift away from obsolete tactics to a trench-style form of combat was necessary.

Rather than try to capture Richmond from north of the James River, Grant decided to come at the Confederate Capital from the south. Petersburg, Virginia, with its five railroad terminals held the key to this maneuver. If captured, Grant could cut off supply lines to Lee. Thus began a nine month long siege. A frontal attack on the Confederates proved disastrous as both sides dug in with trenches enforced with long spear-headed poles protruding outward the length of the fortification. Even planting four tons of explosives in an excavated area under the enemy ended in Union folly as a huge crater trapped thousands of men who became targets—many of them from a recently formed black regiment.

Finally, out-numbered and out-supplied, Lee's forces could no longer hold Petersburg and left it for the Union. Hours later, Richmond fell as well.

One week after the evacuation of Richmond, Lee surrendered to Grant on April 9,1865, at Appomattox Courthouse. Dignity and respect prevailed on both sides as troops lined the walkway to the meeting house. Any emotional victory celebrations were reserved for the evening campfires.

"Hard to believe it's over," said Hans as he sipped his coffee. "Not many of us original troops left in the Twentieth. Most of the officers from Harvard either wounded or dead. We've been lucky, Alex."

"There've been a few times when I wasn't sure we'd make it, but like I told you before, Mammy's a powerful prayer warrior." Alex's countenance grew solemn. "It should have been me who got hit, not Willie. Why her?"

Hans shook his head. "Don't have an answer. I pray she's living at the convent. Can't think of a safer place for her. Soon as I get mustered out of this company, I'm going back to Gettysburg. Can't be that hard to find the nuns."

Alex squeezed his friend's shoulder. "That makes two of us. You didn't think I'd let you go alone, do you? Time to turn in. We may be heading north tomorrow."

***

The celebratory attitude among the troops lasted only five days when news of Lincoln's assassination threw a shroud of gloom over the regiment. Unanswered questions were on everyone's mind. "How could this happen? And in a public theater? What would become of the Union now?"

For the next ten days, men, wagons loaded with supplies, artillery and horses snaked their way through familiar territory, each battle area still fresh in their memories. By the time the Army of the Potomac reached Washington, the city was still draped in black and Lincoln's body was on a train headed to his burial ground in Illinois.

A week later, anxious to be mustered out of the infantry, Hans and Alex surrendered their rifles and caught a train bound for Pennsylvania—destination, Gettysburg. Once there, they inquired of the locals where they could find the convent. After a half-hour buggy ride, nestled among the green hills, they spotted a white clapboard dwelling with a large wooden cross bolted above the entrance. Tying the horse to a fence post, Hans turned to Alex, "What if it isn't Willie? My stomach feels real jittery."

"My heart's beating like crazy, too, but there's only one way to find out, isn't there. C'mon."

"But I never talked to a nun before. I'm nervous. You do the talkin', Alex."

"Alright. I can't stand here another minute."

Before they even had time to knock, the door opened and a woman dressed in a nun's tunic asked, "May I help you?"

Alex stepped up and started the conversation. "Ma'am, my name is Alex McPhail and this is Hans Baden. We're looking for his sister and were told she may be living here. Her name is Winona."

Sister Mary looked the men over, taking note of their Union uniforms and the look of hope in their eyes. "There's no one here except us nuns." Within seconds, she saw hope turn to disappointment and their shoulders no longer stood tall. "But there was."

Hans bounced back with eagerness and his shyness evaporated. "You mean my sister was really here?" He turned to Alex and hugged his neck. "She's alive. She's alive. Ma'am, is she well? Where did she go?"

Sister Mary's smile broadened until her face glowed. "My prayers have been answered. Come in gentlemen, we have much to talk about and I know you are famished."

"Amnesia?" exclaimed Hans wiping a dribble of soup from his lips. "After all these months. No wonder she never wrote."

"Yes," said Sister Mary, "and there's another reason." She turned to Alex. "Winona told me about her relationship with you. She thought it better you think she'd died."

"But why?"

"She's afraid you'll no longer want a woman disfigured with half a leg."

"No, that's not true, Sister." Alex's voice revealed passion. "My love for Winona runs deep. We've been through more than you can ever imagine. When I think of the suffering she tolerated..."

His words caught in his throat and his composure faltered. "It puts me to shame. Her wound should have been mine."

A moment of silence passed before Hans spoke up. "You told us she's on a mission to help black woman and children adapt to their new lives. Where is she?"

"Shortly after President Lincoln announced the Emancipation Proclamation, a group of concerned folks formed the United Christian Coalition. Different denominations are represented. Their goal is to travel into the south offering assistance but she didn't know where she'd end up. Of course, with communication as bad as it is, we've lost contact and I don't know when she'll return." Sister Mary sighed, "I haven't been much help, have I?"

"On the contrary, Ma'am, you've given us back hope. Knowing Winona is alive has been worth the journey. I'll be traveling south myself in a few days. Most of the trip will be on the back of a horse since the railways are torn up pretty bad. It's a long shot, but maybe I'll get lucky and find her."

Sister Mary reached out and placed her hand on Alex's arm. "It won't be luck, my son—God's will. Bless you."

***

During the ride back to the train station, Han's exuberance could not be contained. "It's a miracle. My sister is alive. I want to shout it to everyone. Thank God Nathan was willing to help."

"I've been told growing up that our Maker works in mysterious ways. I'll never dispute that— not after this experience."

"So when are you leaving?"

"In gratitude to Uncle Robert, I need to give the family a proper farewell. Then I'm thinking of finding passage on a navy supply ship heading for Charleston. The north is going to have to replenish what we destroyed if there's to be any re-construction."

"How are you going to get to Oak Haven? Rumor has it that Sherman ripped up the rails, heated them up and bent them around the trees. Why not sail to Jacksonville?"

"I'll buy a horse. I want to travel the land and get a first-hand look at the areas we never got near—like Georgia. I hear that General Sherman went above and beyond civility destroying Atlanta. It grieves me to know ordinary citizens took the brunt of this conflict. My eyes have been opened. It's obvious that politicians and the wealthy gentry on both sides did the planning then left the fighting to men like us."

Hans gave the horse a snap of the reins and the wagon gathered speed. "One thing I know. I've heard enough boomin', roaring and screamin' to last me the rest of my life. I'm thinkin' of joining the merchant marines and sail around the world. Boston Harbor's one of their ports. Now that I know my sister is in good hands, I believe I'll do just that."

"Sounds like a great adventure. Let the four winds rid your memory of the last four years, not that you'll ever forget, but at least it'll be a change of scene."

Chapter Forty-five

Not only did Alex want to say good-bye to his northern family, but he wanted to take Robert into his confidence. After a private conversation, he said, "I'm as surprised as you are, Uncle. Never did I expect to find my soul mate in a Union uniform, fighting alongside me as bravely as any soldier on the field."

Robert, stunned by this turn of events, replied, "Are you certain you aren't chasing the wind, son? War can heighten feelings that otherwise may not be there when life returns to normal—especially now that this woman is crippled."

Alex leaned forward. "Let me ask you a question. "Did you have any doubts when you married Aunt Abigail?"

Robert smiled as a twinkle danced in his eyes, "Not a one. I'd do it again tomorrow."

A chuckle proceeded Alex's comment. "I thought as much. Uncle, I won't be content until I find Winona." He paused, took a long breath and continued, "I hesitate to ask this because you've done so much for me…"

"What is it?"

"I'm going to send Sister Mary at the Sisters of Mercy convent in Gettysburg a letter requesting that she write you as soon as Winona returns. I'm hopeful that mail delivery will commence in a few months, but if not, at least you will know her whereabouts and somehow we can communicate."

Robert looked with intensity at his nephew. " Alex, I see the conviction in your eyes that you had when you first joined the army. I trust it will stay with you the rest of your life. When a man is passionate about whatever is dear to him, it always shows. I'll be honored to help you."

***

Outfitted in a new suit of clothes, a journal book, and some food provisions, Alex boarded a ship bound for Charleston. As he headed south, his mind had difficulty making the transformation from soldier to civilian. He dreamed he was riding into battle again and kept looking out for skirmishers and sharp shooters. Scenes of former battles brought nightmares and always he heard Willie's screams in the background.

During the day, he sat near the bow of the ship savoring the warmth of the sun and the smell of fresh salty air. Here, he began writing in a journal. *Who knows, maybe someday my future children will want to know what happened these past four years to drive a wedge through our country. I'll tell them the truth as I experienced it.*

The first line of Alex's journal began: I've come full-circle. I started north on a ship in April, 1861 and I'm returning September, 1865 on one of the same, but with one exception. I was an impressionable, energetic lad when I left Oak Haven; I come home a war-weary, mature man. Although I'm convinced I did the right thing in joining the Army of the Potomac to preserve the Union, I'll do everything in my power to help unite the shattered southern lives of those who stood bravely for their convictions.

In the coming days, I shall leave this ship and travel the land by horse and foot, for in my mind, it's the only way I'll understand the heartache and pain inflicted upon citizens who have suffered. Maybe I feel a tinge of guilt for their circumstances. But I did my job and now I want to define my new mission.

***

What used to be a slave auction area in the heart of Charleston, now became a livestock auction. After examining horse after horse, Alex bought a sturdy looking mare. A near-by tack shop supplied him with the necessary riding gear and a blanket. Few food supplies were available in town, but he'd saved the salted meat, the canned fish and a box of crackers given to him by Bessie. A canteen of fresh water hung around his shoulders.

It was obvious to Alex as he rode through the countryside into Georgia that Sherman's men did everything in their power to destroy property and civilian livelihoods. He saw fields in uncultivated shambles while others were burned, homes left gutted of all valuables, and plantations had a ghost-like presence, devoid of emancipated slaves.

At each town Alex entered, he first looked for a church or public building and inquired if a group of men and women had been there to offer help. Often his inquiry was met with rebuke.

"You one of those carpet baggers who's come down here to pretend to be our friend. Trouble—that's all you want. Ain't satisfied we lost the war and are left with nothin'. Now you want whatever you can steal. Take my advice fancy pants, git out'a town before you git run out."

Alex took heed. *No sense surviving four years of the worst fighting this country ever saw to be shot by some disenchanted Rebel.*

Covering twenty miles a day, sleeping in abandoned fields under the stars by night, Alex made slow but steady progress toward Oak Haven. Even though his father would not be there, he still felt the sting of his rejection. *Will the others treat me as family again or as an outsider? Oh well, I guess I'll soon find out.*

At Columbus, Georgia, an ember of hope ignited Alex's search for Willie. A sign posted by the courthouse caught his attention. 'Volunteers needed to help the United Christian Coalition'. "That's Willie's group," he muttered out loud.

"Sir," a gentle voice from behind, interrupted his enthusiasm.

Alex turned to face a black woman carrying a basket of melons. "They ain't here no more. Moved on about a month ago."

"Where did they go?" Words came rushing out of his crestfallen mouth.

"Don't know. All's they say is they help us as long as they could and haf to go south. Sure miss 'em. I know my letters an numbers now. And I can sew pretty good, too."

"Tell me, was there a young woman with yellow hair with them. She walks with a crutch."

The whites of the woman's eyes grew large and a big smile revealed ivory-colored teeth. "Oh Lawdy, Miss Winona her name. Poor soul. Lost a leg fightin' for my freedom. She one special lady."

Alex could barely contain his joy. "Yes, yes, she is. Think, ma'am, are you sure you don't remember their destination?"

Her bandana-covered head lowered and Alex noted she closed her eyes. After a moment, she looked at him and said, "I sorry, sir, but I's thinks and thinks. Never heard where they go. You a friend?"

"Yes."

"Well, you keeps a'lookin', you hear. She worth findin'." With that, she pulled a melon from the basket and offered it to Alex. "Here. It make a fine supper."

"Thank you, ma'am. You've given me more than you realize. God bless."

"He do, sir. Indeed, He do."

Chapter Forty-six

For the next two weeks, Alex searched every town or hamlet he rode through for any clue of the mission group's activity. No one had heard of such an organization. By now familiar landscape beckoned him home. He felt the pull and was relieved to see that Florida was not the scorched earth attributed to other states that seceded. Though cotton crops wilted in the fields, he still saw remnants of slaves who chose to remain on the plantations. *How did Oak Haven fare?*

By day's end, he wondered no more. Ahead of him, in the dim of the evening, stood the 'big house' at the end of the brick-covered lane. Home at last. Alex pulled on the reins. The horse snorted and came to a stop. One small light shone in a lone window. Nervous tremors in the pit of his stomach held Alex from galloping up to the entrance. *Will they even recognize me?*

Taking a deep breath, he nudged the horse on until he could go no further. Alex secured the reins to a porch column, walked up the steps and knocked on the door.

He heard the scuffling of a chair and then the door opened a crack. Light from a candle illuminated his sister's beloved face.

"May I help you?" she asked.

Alex couldn't resist the tease in his reply. "Only if you want to see your brother?"

"Alex!" The door swung open. "Mammy come quick. It's Alex!"

Sue Ellen disposed of the candle and flung her arms around her brother's neck, hugging and kissing every inch of his face.

Out of the shadows came Mammy, her arms ready to gather

her own like a mother hen. Smothered in affection, any fear of rebuff Alex felt vanished.

Both women, full of questions gave Alex little time to catch his breath. Finally, he asked, "Joshua? Is he still here?"

"He never left." Mammy took his hand and led him to the kitchen. "He got big plans for you. Wait 'til you see him. He at a Freedmen's Bureau meetin' tonight."

She hugged his neck again. "I'm so happy you back home and now I can cook for you. Look Sue Ellen. Ain't your brother skinny as my broom? Well, Mammy take care of that." Before Alex could respond, she went to the cupboard and got out biscuits, eggs and ham. "Now don't tell me you ain't hungry 'cause I knows better. Talk to your sister. I leave you two alone."

Alex saw aging lines on his sister's face and threads of gray mixed in with her auburn hair. "It's been tough for you, hasn't it, sis?"

Sue Ellen nodded. "Especially when Andrew died. It was such a shock when Uncle Robert handed me his ring and Bible. But how thankful I am you were with him. Did he suffer long? I wake up with that question haunting me. As you know, he was a gentle man—war was not his nature but when the call went out for more recruits, he told me it was his duty."

Alex patted Sue Ellen's hand as he dispelled her qualms. "He was in the field hospital when I found him. He went quickly and you were on his mind right to the last. So much has happened to me these past four years. Terrible things and wonderful things. But tonight, let's just forget about the war and enjoy each other."

***

Alex swallowed the last bite of his third biscuit when Joshua walked into the kitchen. Neither Mammy nor Sue Ellen said a word but let each man recognize the other. In one simultaneous movement, they wrapped arms around each other as Joshua spoke, "Thank God you're home, Alex. No missin' limbs or bullet holes?"

"A slight graze but that's past history." Alex stood back and sized up his friend. "Hey, how'd you get taller than me? And heavier, too?"

"Mammy's cookin, I reckon."

"You're right. Salt pork and hardtack didn't do much for me, but just give me a couple months and I'll be catchin' up. I still have a wrestling score to settle with you."

Alex noted that Joshua's usual jovial manner was missing and it puzzled him, especially when he looked first at Sue Ellen and then his mother. "There may be more than wrestling to settle. I wants him to know the truth now."

"What truth? Have I missed something since I've been gone?"

"Come sit at the table everyone," motioned Sue Ellen. "Joshua you brought it up, so you go first."

Alex's curiosity peaked. *What's going on?*

"Alex, Mammy has been keeping a secret from the time we was born 'til just before your father died." He paused for a moment. "You and I are half-brothers."

Alex heard soft weeping as the words registered in his mind. " Half-brothers? So Angus McPhail is your father, too? Was it rape, Mammy? I know slave owners are known to take advantage of younger women. Please tell me."

By now tears flowed down her cheeks and her response was a nod. Finally between sobs, she managed to say, "When he take a liken to me, he send my man away. Sold him down at the town square. I never sees him no more."

"But she got even with Father," interjected Sue Ellen. "Mammy came to me after emancipation and told me the whole story. She swore on a Bible in her hand that it was true. She wanted Joshua and I to be witnesses to a confession from Father. They'd had this conversation before she came to me and he refused."

Back in control of herself, Mammy said, "I tells him, 'Either you do as I say, or I be putin' arsenic in your food—little by little.' He knows I be a woman of my word so he agree."

Sue Ellen cut back in, "I wrote a letter of confession for Father to sign. Two days before his death, we three gathered around his bed and witnessed his signature."

"It meant so much to me for my son to know who his real father is."

Joshua joined the conversation. "I understand this is a lot to take on your first night home, but Alex, I got to know if knowing you have a black half-brother changes things between us. We always been best friends."

Alex heard the honesty in Joshua's voice and the pleading in his eyes. *Why should his color change our friendship?* He reached across the table and squeezed his brother's arm. "Nothing between us has changed. Ever since we were kids, I always felt our friendship was special."

"There's something else," Sue Ellen explained. "I checked with a lawyer and since Joshua is a legal son, he is entitled to his share of Father's estate."

"I was disinherited so it doesn't concern me." Alex sat back and folded his arms.

"It does now because Joshua and I had a new will drawn up and you are included."

This time Alex wiped at the tears in his eyes. "I never expected to be part of Oak Haven again."

"We're all family, Alex. Southern kin stick together."

"This is the plan Sue Ellen and I have been workin' on," said Joshua. "The soil here has lost it's minerals. Cotton barely grows anymore. We need to give it a rest. I bin goin' to learn about farming at the Freedmen's Bureau and they says we need to plant soy beans and peanuts. They claim there's money to be had if we do."

"I agree with Joshua that growing cotton isn't what it used to be. What have we got to lose?"

Alex saw excitement light up Sue Ellen's face. *Might be just what she needs to get on with her life.*

"You and me can handle the outside field work and Sue Ellen will handle the money."

"Sounds like a good plan to me," smiled Alex. "When do we start?"

"First, I want to take you over to the Bureau in Tallahassee to show you what I've been learnin'. Thanks to you brother for teachin' me how to read."

Sue Ellen spoke up, " Before you two go wandering all over the county tomorrow, I want Alex to come see what I've been doing."

"And what would that be, sister?"

"There's a group from the north in town who've been traveling around teaching skills to our freed slaves. They call themselves the United Christian Coalition and they need volunteers, so I go to the town hall a couple days a week."

Alex thought his heart would stop and he fought to control his excitement. *Should I tell them about Willie or wait and see for myself if she's there? Too many high hopes have been shattered. I'll wait.*

By now it was far past everyone's bedtime. Sue Ellen asked a prayer of thanks for Alex's safe arrival and good-night hugs were shared by all. As he climbed the familiar stairs to his old bedroom, Alex turned and said to Sue Ellen, "It's been quite a homecoming. Do you have any more surprises?"

"None that I'm aware of, dear brother. How about you?"

"I may have one. I think you'll like it. Good-night."

Chapter Forty-seven

The possibility of finding Willie at the town hall kept Alex in a high state of anxiety most of the night. *Is it over Lord? Will she accept me?* After much tossing and turning, his travel weary body succumbed to deep slumber along with a troubling dream. Over and over he saw Willie screaming at him, "You told me you'd never let anything or anyone hurt me. Take a look at what's left of my leg. Stay away from me. I want nothing more to do with you."

The crow of the rooster wakened him and in the dim morning light it took a few seconds to orient himself to familiar surroundings. Nothing had changed—the furniture, the bedside lamp, the shelf lined with classic books and even a child's wooden rocking horse sat in the corner. On the wall hung a framed printed copy of The Lord's Prayer.

Not wishing to disturb the rest of the household at an early hour, Alex nestled back under the coverings and soon fell asleep again.

Two hours later, he wakened to a knock on his door. "Come in."

Sue Ellen walked over to the bed and gave her brother a morning hug. "I know you're exhausted from all the traveling, but I'm needed at the town hall in an hour or so and I want you to have one of Mammy's wonderful breakfasts before we go."

Alex shook the fuzzy feeling from his head and threw back the covers. "You have no idea how I've missed one of those." He sniffed the air. "Is that bacon I smell and real coffee? Tell her to crack the eggs. I'll be right down."

***

While Sue Ellen gathered a basket of quilting material for the women at the center, Alex hitched his horse to a carriage. In no time, they were on their way into town. As they passed familiar landmarks and neighboring plantations, Sue Ellen brought her brother up to date on the local news.

"There's barely a family around us who hasn't been touched by the loss of a loved one." Her voice faltered as she continued, "War accomplishes nothing but heartache."

Alex reached over and patted her hand. "I can't argue with that, but the wounds of hatred will not heal if left open to fester." Not wishing to dwell on the negative, Alex took their conversation in another direction.

"Tell me more about this United Christian group you've been helping."

The smile that Alex always cherished brought a glow to Sue Ellen's face. "Oh, they've been wonderful—a real God-send to our community. The men are teaching carpentry, husbandry, blacksmith skills and farming to the males out at the old fairgrounds. The women are learning house-hold skills." Sue Ellen pointed to her basket. "I found yards of scrap material in our attic that will make perfect quilt squares. Think of it, when all a person has been allowed to achieve with their hands is picking cotton, most have never learned anything else. If they're ever going to fend for themselves, they need to learn basic skills."

"Joshua was telling me at breakfast that at the Freedman's Bureau there's talk of something new called share cropping. A plot of land is given to those who want to farm for themselves. At the time of harvest a portion is given back to the owner as rent. It seems reasonable to me. We've got plenty of property that could be divided into smaller portions. What do you think?"

"Sounds sensible. With most of our former help gone, there's no way two men can handle it all. It's the folks who are too old to travel long distances and some too feeble to do much physically who stayed. They might be able to handle a small farm."

"You know, Sue Ellen, southern folk may not believe this, but President Lincoln wished to bring the Rebel states back into the

Union with a gentle hand. I believe he realized there had been enough suffering, but thanks to that scoundrel, Booth, we'll never know his full intentions."

"I agree it's a sad mark on our history, although there are many who applaud his death."

"That's what worries me." Alex pulled his hat lower over his forehead, "The guns may be silenced, but I fear those black folk who chose to remain in the south will continue to face opposition—especially from the New Radical Republicans. That group are up to no good. A certain segment of our society are afraid they'll lose power they once enjoyed. It wouldn't surprise me if there aren't lynchings in the near future."

Sue Ellen gasped and grabbed her brother's right arm. "Surely not, but warn Joshua to be careful. He's apt to be noticed with his involvement with the Freedmen's Bureau and his new ideas."

"I'll talk to him about his involvement in such organizations along with his politics. He's a literate black man so that makes him a target for cowards hiding in the shadows. They fear and despise men like him."

A shudder ran through Sue Ellen's body and she changed the subject. " Let me tell you more about this group I'm helping. You must hear how quickly the children are learning the letters and some can even read. Their teacher is a young woman who, bless her soul, hobbles about with a crutch."

Alex could hold his tongue no longer. "What else do you know about her?"

"Not much. I never asked what caused her misfortune because I feel it's a personal matter." Sue Ellen smiled before she continued, "I can see she's an independent sort—nothing holds her back."

You have no idea, my dear sister. No idea. At the thought of Willie, Alex's impatience grew. He snapped the horse's reins and the animal's trot gained momentum. *My precious girl, what will your answer be?*

Chapter Forty-eight

As the wagon moved down the main street of Tallahassee, Alex recognized different shops and hotels, churches and the state capital building. Physically, it looked as though nothing had changed much in his four-year absence, but Alex was prepared to be snubbed, cursed and even spat at by folks he'd known since childhood. *I'm sure Father did nothing to defend his son's actions. Well, they'll just have to get over it because I'm home to stay.*

The clock on the old town hall, struck ten and with each second, Alex felt his heart beat—thump, thump, thump, thump. He wished he could control his body's anxious behavior but it was no use. *I feel like a puppet dancing on a string, and Willie has me in her control. I don't remember ever being this nervous going into battle.* Alex wiped his brow of perspiration then jumped down from the carriage and gave a helping hand to his sister.

The chatter of female conversation echoed in Alex's ears as he entered the main room of the town hall. Sitting around a large quilting frame he saw a group of twelve women each stitching a multi-colored star-burst pattern on a blue background. It was obvious to him that pride of accomplishment shone on each black face as they completed square after square.

One elderly woman turned to her neighbor and said, "I never sleeps under anything so pretty in all my years. We's lucky if we got a tattered ole woolen blanket to keep us warm. Did you ever thinks we'd have a chance to win us such a covering? We's gonna pull numbers when it finished and the winner get to take it with her. If nothin' else, now I knows how to make one of my own."

Sylvia Melvin

While Sue Ellen busied herself with a needle and thread, Alex went in search of Willie. In one room the discussion dealt with the importance of proper hygiene. In another, a volunteer demonstrated the technique of preserving fruits and vegetables. The third, scantily furnished with a table, a blackboard, one chair and a shelf containing several books caught his eye. From within, a familiar sweet laughter stopped him in his tracks. Before him, dressed in a blue gingham dress that flowed from her tiny waist to the floor, stood, supported by a crutch under her left arm, the woman he knew he would love the rest of his life. Eight children sat cross-legged in a semi-circle transfixed by the words flowing from her rosy-red lips.

Alex's first impulse was to rush in and gather her in his arms, but he waited. This was a moment he wanted to savor—her golden strands of hair, no longer shaggy and unruly, but combed back into an elegant braid, the silver locket still hanging around porcelain skin and even yet, the tell-tale scar still visible above her left wrist as she held the book she was reading.

The moment she finished, Alex put his hands together and the sound of clapping filled the room. Startled, the children turned in his direction and then with puzzled faces sought their teacher's reaction.

Alex saw Willie's face grow pale as the crutch slipped from under her arm and hit the floor. Her body went limp and threatened to collapse. With two giant strides, he caught her before she fell.

"A..A...lex." Her words whispered against his cheek. "How did you find me?"

Alex tightened his hold around her waist. "It's a long story but thank God I did. It's been a horrible nightmare. But I never gave up."

Willie pulled back and looked into his eyes. "You should have. I'm not the woman who went with you into battle. I should have taken your advice and given myself up."

"Willie, I know why you carry a crutch. Hans and I were told at the field hospital. Think of all the men who've gone back home to their wives with missing limbs. Do you think I'd stop loving you?"

Even though Willie's eyes were now brimming with tears, she found his lips and sealed her answer. Squeals of laughter and giggles erupted from the children and soon attracted the attention of some of the women.

"Alex?" exclaimed Sue Ellen as the couple drew back from each other. "I was planning on introducing you two but..."

"We've met dear sister. It's a story I can't wait to tell you, but not now. We'll have to let Mammy know there'll be another place at the table for supper tonight."

Alex looked at Willie and said, "I'm hoping it'll be a permanent one."

The smile she gave him set his pulse racing.

***

Leaving Sue Ellen and Willie to get acquainted, Alex returned to Oak Haven to find Joshua. His first stop was the kitchen where Mammy, busy kneading biscuits for the evening meal, took one look at his beaming face. "That not the Alex I sees this mornin'. You hidin' somethin'. Now you knows you never could keep secrets from me."

"Mammy, this is the best day of my life. I finally found the woman I intend to marry."

Mammy's eyes grew big and her brows arched in surprise as she placed her floured hands on her hips. "What you say? Son, you ain't bin home not a full day and already you finds a wife? Lawdy, the war done take away your sense."

Alex exploded in laughter. "She's coming for supper, too."

"Tonight?"

"And for many nights after, I hope."

Mammy wiped her hands on her apron and motioned toward the table. "Come sit. We gots to talk. This serious business. Now, tell me 'bout this woman."

For the next hour, Alex described the events that brought he and Willie together and the heartache he felt when he thought all was lost.

Mammy wiped rolling tears from her cheeks with the corner of her apron then took Alex's hands in hers. "God bless her soul. I never hears of a woman fightin' for my freedom. She sure welcome in this home." Mammy gave Alex her best smile and kissed his right hand. " I sees the happiness and peace you feel at findin' your mate. It must be like the Bible say when a man and woman be yoked together in faith, ain't nothin' gonna tear them apart."

Alex squeezed Mammy's fingers in appreciation of her blessing just as the screen door opened. Joshua looked at Alex and with a tease said, "Hey, brother, I know you've been away for four years but we got work to do. I saddled up Starlight so let's get on over to the Bureau. There's lots we can talk about on the way."

Mammy gave Joshua a sly grin. "Oh, son, you ain't heard nothin' yet. You let Alex do the talkin'. Off with you both." As Alex picked up his hat she said, "There'll be an extra plate on the table tonight. You can count on it."

***

The wedding, two weeks later, was small in attendance, but the love that radiated among the participants set the tone for a new future. After the celebration, the newlyweds cuddled up on the porch swing and watched the sun go down.

Alex tilted Willie's chin toward him and kissed her waiting lips. "I'd go through it all again for this moment. I know I took Winona Baden as my wife, but to me you'll always be Willie. We've been through the worst of times, and there may still be struggles ahead, but I'm convinced our children will be part of a world we fought for the day we picked up our rifles—a country united from north to south."

The End

About the Author

Sylvia Melvin lives in Milton, Florida. She is an Elementary School Intervention teacher.

Her Canadian heritage is often reflected in her writing. She enjoys writing short stories, biographies, romance and mysteries.

As one of the founding members of the Panhandle Writer's Group, she is motivated by her fellow writers and the skills she has learned.

Sylvia likes to take her readers to places they've never visited, meet folks who arouse their emotions and leave them wanting to read more.

***

If you would like to write a short review of this book, *Convictions,* please feel free to do so. Simply go to Amazon.com and type in "Convictions Sylvia Melvin" in the search bar. Scroll down to the reviews section.

Thank you for your interest.

Made in the
USA
Columbia, SC

81916158R00133